Today's Journey Tarot

A Traveler's Guide

Today's Journey Tarot

A Traveler's Guide

By

Expanding Dimensions

Illustrated by

Christopher Wilkey

R. C. Linnell Publishing

TODAY'S JOURNEY TAROT A TRAVELER'S GUIDE

© Copyright 2013 by Expanding Dimensions and Licensors

All rights reserved. No part of this book may be reproduced or used for any reason or by anyone with permission. The only exception being small excerpts from the book that will be used to glorify and promote it.

Cover design by Dave Davis
Illustrated by Christopher Wilkey
Photos by Joy Vest

ISBN 10: 09840025-6-1
ISBN 13: 978-0-9840025-6-6

Published by:
R.C. Linnell Publishing
Louisville, KY 40205
www.LinnellPublishing.com

Other publications by Expending Dimensions:
Today's Journey Tarot (card deck) ISBN: 978-0-7643-3905-9
www.TodaysJourneyTarot.com

This book is dedicated to all the travelers on

Today's Journey:

those who kept the wisdom alive,

those living it today,

and those yet to discover it.

CONTENTS

Introduction 1

Introduction to the Keys 6

    Keys 11

Introduction to the Elements 45

    Fire 51

    Water 71

    Air 91

    Earth 111

Layouts 131

    One Card Readings 132

    Three Card Readings 133

    Today's Celtic Cross 138

    Seven Card Merkaba Spread 140

Reading the Tarot 143

Meditating with the Tarot 165

Numbers, Colors and Symbols 173

Biographies 179

Conclusion 183

INTRODUCTION

Life is a series of cycles continuously beginning, ending, and beginning again. We are all travelers on this journey, looking for answers to guide our way and understand our place in the wheel of life. The first twenty-two cards of the Tarot, often referred to as the Major Arcana or Keys describe the steps that are necessary to successfully move from one cycle to another. Throughout history this knowledge has been kept hidden or known only to a few. It was shrouded in ritual and mystery, difficult to understand and interpret. Today this veil has been lifted.

The members of Expanding Dimensions started reading and studying the Tarot many years ago. Over those years, we've done it all: private readings, psychic fairs, lectures, demonstrations and ultimately teaching the Tarot to others. We started out as seekers and have become teachers. We love the cards and their ancient wisdom that resonates deeply with everything we believe. We have all used a variety of decks and collected others, but always returned to the classic Rider/Waite/Smith deck because it seemed to express the concepts best. One of the things that became apparent to all of us is this deck is dated. After all, the world was very different in 1910 when it was published. Some of the images frighten people because they have become associated with negative outcomes, such as the "Devil" card or "Death." Many students complained that it was too difficult to learn what the unfamiliar symbols on the cards represented. Oftentimes, those who stuck with it ended up memorizing book meanings or other's interpretations of the cards rather than actually interpreting for themselves. This limits the Tarot's contribution to a reading. Just like any tool, it expresses the skill and knowledge of the one using it and having someone else tell you the meaning of a thing is quite different from learning on your own. We felt that there should be a deck that was easy to read and understand and yet still retained the symbolism of ancient archetypes to convey the esoteric meaning of each card to those who were using them. We also wondered why there were so many decks out there with a myriad of themes but nothing that addressed these truths in simple and direct language. We believed that truth does not have to be hidden behind obscure symbolism. It should be available to all. It is only hidden when we make it hidden.

So we decided to design a new Tarot deck to see if a twenty first century deck depicting everyday life could offer everything an esoteric deck could. Today's Journey Tarot does just that. Over the next eight years, we conceived each of the seventy eight images through group discussion and debate. Each card was envisioned and then described on paper. We chose the colors, symbols, characters and their activities in fine detail. We decided each suit should be represented in its most basic form, the element it symbolizes. Those suits are Fire, Water, Air and Earth. The Major Arcana has always been known as Keys. Why not call them that? Our one esoteric indulgence is the symbol of the merkaba, a vehicle to reach enlightenment. This symbol is the back design and is repeated throughout the deck. A merkaba consists of two equally sized, interlocked tetrahedra (pyramids) with a common center, where one tetrahedron points up and the other down. "Mer" means light. "Ka" means spirit. "Ba" means body. The merkaba is a spirit body of light. This symbol of transformation epitomizes our belief in the power of the Tarot.

It was an inspired collective vision. At first, our only intention was to further our own search for knowledge, but soon it became an entity with its own voice. Eventually we decided to engage an illustrator to capture the concepts in actual images. He took our descriptions and interpreted our vision into individual works of art.

Today's Journey Tarot was published in 2011. When we show the cards to people who have never read before, they can instantly describe what is going on and what it may mean. Someone jumping off a cliff in a hang glider is probably a risk taker, someone who is independent and maybe a bit reckless. A girl sitting with her back to the pole of her mailbox, staring off down the road is waiting and must be patient until what she's waiting for arrives. A woman in a fur coat admiring herself in a mirror could be somewhat self-absorbed or attached to material things. We can identify with the images and apply them to our own lives. Are we being too reckless in a situation? Should we wait a while and not act right now? Are we too worried about status quo and missing out on the simple joys of life? We believe this deck is an answer for all of the people who have been drawn to the Tarot cards and not been able to read them. This deck does not require memorization of seventy eight different cards and hundreds of symbols before you can begin using them. You don't have to be trained in esoteric wisdom or learn the glyphs for ancient concepts. You just sit down and read for yourself or for others. The common sense and beauty of the Tarot pours forth.

The origins of the Tarot are a mystery. Rumors about the deck's history have been debated for years. We simply do not know for certain where the deck originated, how old it is, or even if the original conception of the system was a deck of cards. The only truth we have is the Tarot itself and the insights it offers into every aspect of human experience. These insights include some of the techniques to effectively move through the cycles of life: learning to meditate, developing intuition, trusting inner guidance, and releasing the ego's control. The Tarot is a vital tool we need, not only to understand the changes in life, but to navigate them successfully. Could this be the reason the Tarot was created in the first place? The Tarot teaches universal truth. Why should it not be available to everyone?

Today's Journey Tarot came out of an idea to learn more about the concepts expressed in the Tarot by conveying those ideas in a contemporary way. There are five of us who toiled together over eight years to give a fresh voice to this tool of enlightenment. We had highs and lows. We struggled and triumphed. There were times when we questioned if we should continue. But always there was the Tarot, leading us and guiding us and never wavering from its encouragement.

IN THIS BOOK

- ❖ Beneath each card's title is a statement of wisdom the card expresses. It is followed by a list of the primary concepts associated with its meaning. These sections are provided as a quick reference for each card.

- ❖ For more in depth study we have included detailed descriptions of the card, commentary about symbolic meanings and interpretation, and expanded card meanings when used in a reading.

- ❖ Following these sections is a meditation for each card. This is a statement of affirmation to be used as a focal point in contemplation for personal growth or for further understanding of the card.

- ❖ If you like to pull a card each morning for a forecast, we have added the card's meaning for a daily reading. This will give you insight into the advantages or the obstacles to look out for that day.

Discover other uses for the Tarot such as meditation, spiritual guidance, and self analysis. We have also included some of our favorite layouts including an expanded version of Today's Journey Tarot's Seven Card Merkaba Spread.

Over the years the members of Expanding Dimensions have been asked many questions about the Tarot. We have included a section with our answers.

After many requests, Today's Journey Tarot, A Traveler's Guide was written for further study of the deck and Tarot in general. Experience has taught us not to doubt the Tarot's wisdom. It has been a trusted companion and councilor. We know it has changed our lives and believe it can do the same for you. Open yourself to the Tarot and allow it to be your guide on Today's Journey.

Expanding Dimensions

Introduction to the Keys

The first twenty two cards of Today's Journey Tarot are called Keys. Often this section is referred to as the Major Arcana, from the Latin for Greater Secrets. They describe the steps that are necessary to successfully move through life's journey from one cycle to another. The Keys represent universal forces such as synchronicity, serendipity, karma/dharma, and yin/yang. The indigo borders of these cards indicate their spiritual significance and the number twenty two, a master number, represents their ancient wisdom. As we progress along our path through these cycles we have experiences that lead to different levels of comprehension.

All journeys begin with a single step.

Beginning is the start of this journey. The traveler is filled with curiosity, seeing the future as a mystery, waiting to be explored. At **Manifestation**, the traveler realizes that life's experiences do not happen simply by chance. The decisions and actions of today help to create what occurs tomorrow. Armed with this insight, the traveler ventures forward unaware of the secrets the Universe has yet to disclose. There is always more knowledge hidden than can ever be known. This understanding is true **Wisdom**. **Creativity** fuels the traveler's imagination, allowing manifestation without restriction until the Traveler is faced with a new truth. Free will does exist, but not outside of natural law. **Law** discloses that the Universe has structure and boundaries. The traveler turns to the reliable comfort of **Tradition**, but it is rigid and does not allow for growth. A voice inside begins to stir. **Union** whispers a suggestion.

The answers cannot be found outside the self, but within, through a Divine connection. The self imposed obstacles that lay on the path ahead will be diminished if the ego can be kept under **Control**. This task is not easy but there is a well of strength within that is always available and inexhaustible if the traveler can learn to tap into **Fortitude**. In **Guidance**, the traveler finds the solution to this difficulty by being open to the direction offered by the Universe. The traveler has discovered that the path is not a smooth straight line. In **Life**, there are hills to climb and challenges to overcome. Without them, there would be no growth. The solution is to balance the positive and negative energies in the Universe as shown in **Karma.** One cannot exist without the other. The traveler now has the opportunity to make a **Choice**. Take the guidance offered and move forward or remain stagnant. **Transition** indicates that no matter what the decision, change is unavoidable. The tools offered by the Universe serve to make the transitions smoother. One of these tools, **Discernment** provides the balance and focus necessary to remain on the path. In an effort to maintain control, the ego creates the illusion of security and the fear to look beyond this delusion as demonstrated by **Materialism**. To create cracks in this façade and help restore balance the Universe must employ an **Intervention**. The traveler begins to realize that the inner and outer worlds do not exist separately. **Meditation** teaches that everything comes from within. Tapping into that inner source of **Intuition**, the traveler begins to trust the flow of information. This trust creates freedom and **Illumination**. It is liberation from the shackles of fear that the ego created. Through this journey of growth, the traveler has achieved a shift in **Awareness**, seeing the world differently than most. There is a Divine presence that exists in all things. At the **Completion** of this cycle the traveler is compelled to share the lessons learned on the journey to help others find their own freedom. The traveler prepares for the next cycle to begin.

Following the traveler's path enables us to understand the significant steps that need to be considered on Today's Journey. We must strive to maintain balance, rely on an inner source of strength and wisdom, release the ego's control of reality, and manifest responsibly in cooperation with natural law. By using these cards as tools we become consciously aware of the cycles, how they work and our place along the path.

Today's Journey Tarot Keys	Traditional Tarot's Major Arcana
Key 0 Beginning	0 The Fool
Key 1 Manifestation	I The Magician
Key 2 Wisdom	II The High Priestess
Key 3 Creativity	III The Empress
Key 4 Law	IV The Emperor
Key 5 Tradition	V The Hierophant
Key 6 Union	VI The Lovers
Key 7 Control	VII The Chariot
Key 8 Fortitude	VIII Strength
Key 9 Guidance	IX The Hermit
Key 10 Life	X Wheel of Fortune
Key 11 Karma	XI Justice
Key 12 Choice	XII The Hanged Man
Key 13 Transition	XIII Death
Key 14 Discernment	XIV Temperance
Key 15 Materialism	XV The Devil
Key 16 Intervention	XVI The Tower
Key 17 Meditation	XVII The Star
Key 18 Intuition	XVIII The Moon
Key 19 Illumination	XIX The Sun
Key 20 Awareness	XX Judgement
Key 21 Completion	XXI The World

Keys

Key 0 Beginning

The simplest action can lead to the most profound discovery.

Primary Concepts: Leap of Faith, New Beginning, Journey of Discovery

Description: Key 0 shows a young woman on the floor of her dorm room with her new deck of Tarot cards. She has just opened the box and has dealt the first five Keys face up in front of her. In her left hand she holds the deck face down. Her right hand is in the process of turning over the next card. Surrounding her are the colors of the four elements of nature: red, blue, yellow, and green. Her cat sits beside her with one paw on her leg.

Commentary: This card suggests the anticipation of a new adventure. The student is experiencing the Tarot on her own for the first time. There is so much to learn and discover at this point, but, of course, she doesn't know that. She holds the cards in her left/receiving hand indicating that she's open to the Tarot's wisdom. The red pennant hanging above her symbolizes fire's primal creative force. The blue floor, like the water element it represents reflects her heightened emotions of excitement and expectation. The green rug beneath her, the color of the earth supports her new growth. Yellow for the air element represents her willingness to learn. These four colors are also interwoven threads throughout the sweater she wears, reinforcing she has everything she needs for her journey. She has the strength of her foundation and the potential for growth.

The cat encourages her to take this journey because he knows, as all animals instinctively do, the journey is life itself. Without the thrill of new beginnings and the learning we experience along the way, life would indeed be boring. The Key's number, 0 The Cosmic Egg, represents the powerful moment in time just before action is taken, the pause before the leap.

IN A READING: Embrace the adventure and be open to new thoughts, ideas, and experiences. This card represents a new journey, a choice, or a new beginning. It often signifies a new spiritual path or inner discovery. This type of change will alter the course of your life. Faith is required to make this choice. Reason tells you not to, but listen to the inner instinctual part of yourself. Be aware that guidance and assistance is available along the way. If you choose not to embrace this change, recognize the choice is also a new beginning.

MEDITATION: I am open to inner wisdom and new discoveries.

DAILY READING: Today is a day for opportunities. Be open to new experiences, ideas, and choices. Don't be afraid to leap.

Key 1 Manifestation

You have the power to change.

Primary Concepts: Conscious Manifestation, Creation, Action

Description: In Key 1, a professor writes a complex equation on the chalkboard. The equation includes the magical symbols for fire, water, air, earth, infinity and the merkaba. The lab table in the foreground displays the reference materials he uses for his work: the tree of life, the golden spiral, other geometric symbols, books, notes and equations. He stands with his back to us with his right hand extended to the board and his left hand down at his side.

Commentary: Like the professor, we have what we need to manifest our reality. Everything has been provided for us. The elements of nature give us the physical structure necessary for life. The merkaba offers us the link to the Divine. It depicts two interlocking pyramids, one facing up and one facing down. The only things to do are actively and consciously participate in harmony with the Universe to have whatever is desired. As the infinity sign or lemniscate over his head suggests, there are no limits. We are doing it right now in our own personal laboratories. We are already masters of manifestation or we would not exist in the physical world. With every thought, word, or deed we are creating the reality of our tomorrows. The professor's white lab coat indicates the purity of his intent. The green board represents the growth he is capable of achieving. The position of his hands reinforce the "as above, so below" symbolism of the merkaba, a vehicle for transformation. The number 1 represents the self, where the power of creation resides.

IN A READING: You have everything you need right now to achieve your goals. It is time to take action. This card is saying that you become an active participant in the creation of your own life instead of just an observer and reactor. All of the tools are at your disposal but conscious manifestation requires awareness and action. You created the situation you are in with your past thoughts, words, and deeds. If you do not like where you are, you have the power to change it by first changing your thoughts.

MEDITATION: I now have the awareness to actively manifest.

DAILY READING: Today is a day for action. Take a step toward fulfilling your goal.

KEY 2 WISDOM

Wisdom is elusive and must be sought.

PRIMARY CONCEPTS: Secrets, Hidden Knowledge, Unseen

DESCRIPTION: Key 2 shows a woman preparing to read the Tarot cards. She sits at a dark wooden table with a gold curtain behind her. Her dress is light blue and she wears a silver cross necklace with equal arms. The cards are laid out on a purple scarf etched with a six pointed star or merkaba layout. There are seven cards face down on the scarf. Her left hand is resting on the deck.

COMMENTARY: Tarot cards are an endless source of inspiration and guidance. This card expresses the need to seek wisdom. It is elusive and is rarely bestowed upon us without effort. Key 2 says while hidden, wisdom is not unattainable. Ask the right questions, be open to new possibilities and accept the answers. That is not always an easy thing to do, but the wisdom remains. We can use whatever method we are comfortable with to go back again and again until we uncover, layer by layer, our own truth. The gold curtain represents the veiled presence of Divine influence, her blue dress, the profound peace that allows awareness to come forth. Her silver equal armed cross suggests balance and intuitive truth. The layout cloth is purple, denoting mastery. Its design is in the shape of a merkaba, a vehicle of enlightenment. Her left or receptive hand rests upon the deck. She trusts that the answers she seeks can be found there. The Key's number, 2 represents cooperation or partnership. The reader is working in harmony with the Tarot to find answers.

IN A READING: Seek answers or spiritual guidance. Don't give up. The information you are looking for is available. It may be hidden right now, but you can uncover it. There are aspects to the current situation that you are not aware of. Secrets may be revealed.

MEDITATION: I am open to truth and will not give up until I find it.

DAILY READING: Today is the day to find answers. Truths are revealed and secrets uncovered.

KEY 3 CREATIVITY

Creativity is the harvest of a fertile mind.

PRIMARY CONCEPTS: Fertility, Birth, Imagination

DESCRIPTION: Key 3 depicts a young, mother-to-be in a nursery. She is wearing denim jeans, a purple shirt, and is barefoot. She is putting up a wallpaper chair rail with the design of toy blocks. These blocks have the letters of the DNA strands. They are G, A, T, and C. She has painted the walls a light green. Yellow furniture, covered in clear plastic can also be seen in the room.

COMMENTARY: This card represents creative expression. Not only is the woman pregnant, the ultimate creative expression, she is also using her creativity to make an environment for her child that will stimulate growth and imagination. Her blue and purple clothing suggests an imaginative spirit and a subconscious connection. The woman's bare feet are firmly grounded to the earth and demonstrate her lack of convention. The DNA strands are the building blocks of life where all creativity is manifest. Green, the color of the walls, encourages growth and abundance. The intellect, represented by the yellow furniture, is covered but not completely obscured. That part of her is there when needed, but it is not the dominant force in her life at this time. The Key's number, 3 is the number of creation. It is self expression, artistry and imagination.

IN A READING: It is time to use your imagination to create what you want in your life. It could involve new ideas, new projects, new associations or whatever you can dream. It is a productive energy that can generate unlimited possibilities. This is a fertile period and could even represent a physical pregnancy.

MEDITATION: I am a creator. I have the ability to make my dreams come true.

DAILY READING: Today is a good day to start new projects. If you can see it, you can produce it.

KEY 4 LAW

Even in perceived chaos there is order.

PRIMARY CONCEPTS: Universal Law, Immutable, Order, Foundation, Acceptance

DESCRIPTION: Key 4 shows a formal garden with green grasses and shrubs sculpted into geometric designs. In the middle of the garden is an armillary supported by a white marble pillar. A gardener, wearing a blue shirt, stands with his right hand resting on the armillary. He is focused on it. In his left hand he holds a garden tool.

A Golden Retriever sits at the man's feet, looking up at him. They are on a white stone path.

COMMENTARY: This card expresses Universal Law. Just as the gardener has kept this garden in perfect order, there is a design to the Universe that never changes. The armillary, which sits at a crossroads, charts the stars and planets as they move in their fixed patterns. The gardener's job is to preserve order by maintaining the plants he oversees. His sky blue shirt represents the peacefulness found when all things are in balance, his pants and shoes, the stability of the earth. The armillary features a fleur-de-lis design. Its three petals symbolize the union of body, mind, and spirit necessary for perfect harmony. The white stone pillar is the law's foundation and the white path is humanity's. The color suggests purity, which does not discriminate. The dog represents the natural world that is also governed by immutable order. This law is so absolute that every kingdom; animal, plant, and mineral are subject to it. The Key's number, 4 symbolizes stability. It is the strength and endurance of the physical world.

IN A READING: Everything in the Universe is as it should be. You may not like it and may not agree, but that is just the way it is. It is important not to fight against that which cannot change. Acceptance is the key. Trust in this law that has kept order for millenniums and learn to work with it. Accept things as they are. You have a strong foundation that will always support you.

MEDITATION: I live in harmony with Universal Law.

DAILY READING: Go with the flow today. Do not resist what you cannot change.

Key 5 Tradition

It is impossible to grow without change.

Primary Concepts: Orthodox Thought, Dogmatic Principles, Cultural Norms

Description: Key 5 shows a yellow stone building with a red domed roof and multi-colored stained glass windows. It sits elevated from the road and separated from the green grass by a white sidewalk. The recessed door is the same dark color as the stone foundation. There are gray clouds in the blue sky above.

Commentary: So much of our society is influenced by one tradition or another. This is not necessarily a bad thing. There are family traditions, religious traditions, political traditions, and on and on. Customs serve to set foundations for the very fabric of our society. The difficulty comes when tradition takes the place of growth. Blindly following cultural norms in rigid adherence does not allow for growth. Society must adapt as times change and humanity progresses. Every generation has to challenge its conventions or it becomes stagnant and irrelevant. Traditions evolve as we become aware and enlightened. The yellow stone of the building represents a rigid mind set; the red dome is a symbol of power and prestige. The colored glass in the windows stands in contrast to the cold structure of the stone symbolizing that the potential for enlightenment is always present even in the most rigid circumstances. This symbolism is repeated above in the blue sky of spirituality breaking through the gray clouds of doubt and fear. The green grass represents growth and the white sidewalk, purity. They are separated from the structure by the dark stone foundation. The entrance is even further removed. The building is set above the road to give the impression of authority. The Key's number, 5 symbolizes humanity's flexibility and freedom to change.

IN A READING: Examine with an open mind your thoughts and principles to determine what are valid and what may be limiting your enlightenment. Blindly following tradition is like sleepwalking through life and letting others make choices for you. Break with traditions or find new traditions. Question old ideas. You may be influenced by someone else and their beliefs that are not your own.

MEDITATION: I am not afraid to be myself.

DAILY READING: Today is the day to break with tradition. Do something new that you've wanted to do but didn't feel like you could.

KEY 6 UNION

The Divine is within everything.

PRIMARY CONCEPTS: Lovers, Connection to Divine, Conscious/Subconscious/Superconscious

DESCRIPTION: Key 6 depicts a couple on a blanket under a star filled sky. They are in a grassy field with a stream and hills in the background. The man is sitting cross-legged with his left hand turned palm down on his knee. His right hand is turned palm up reaching towards the woman and he is looking up at her. He is wearing khaki pants. The woman stands beside him with her head slightly turned away from him to her right. Her gaze is directed toward the star cluster known as the Pleiades. She is reaching down with her left hand to grasp his. Her right hand is facing up. She is wearing a gauzy dress. They are both barefoot.

COMMENTARY: This card expresses one of the most important philosophies of the Tarot. The Divine is reached through prayer, meditation or contemplation, not through rational thought alone. The man represents the conscious mind, thought, which is always striving to find its meaning in the universe. The woman, who represents the subconscious or intuition, shows him the way by reaching out to the superconscious Universe. The logical, earth bound part of us must learn to trust our intuitive, Divine self in order to truly experience the wisdom and truths of spirituality. The couple is part of the natural world represented by the field, stream and hills around them as well as their clothes. Their bare feet ground them to this physical environment. The infinite starry sky suggests the realm of the Divine. His left hand receives the earth's energy. Her right hand receives the energy of the Universe. Their hands, reaching for each other form the link that creates the cycle of spiritual growth. In the woman's line of sight are the Pleiades, the seven star cluster in the constellation Taurus that is rich with its own symbolism and is an influence for awakening consciousness. When the mental mind focuses on the Tarot images a link to the superconscious is engaged opening the mind to unlimited possibilities. The Key's number 6 represents harmony and relationships.

IN A READING: When the balance of the equal union of body, mind, and spirit is achieved, you will know the answers you seek. This card says that it is time for you to make that search to recognize and accept your own spirituality. It can also represent a new union either within or outside yourself. It could be a lover, friendship, a business partnership, or a spiritual guide. This is an important relationship.

MEDITATION: I create the balance of body, mind, and spirit.

DAILY READING: Today is a powerful day to make connections. Be open to new opportunities for partnership, friendship, or love.

KEY 7 CONTROL

Self discipline is freedom, not limitation.

PRIMARY CONCEPTS: The Conscious Will, Self Discipline, Triumph, Travel

DESCRIPTION: Key 7 depicts a man on a yellow bicycle. He is going down hill on a curvy mountain road, dressed for riding with black shorts, a blue sleeveless shirt, a helmet and sunglasses, and fingerless gloves. On his shirt is the Pleiades star cluster introduced in Key 6, Union. He is not holding on to the handlebars. His arms are waving up in the air and he has a huge smile on his face.

COMMENTARY: The rider controls the bike with his will, not with his hands. He has allowed himself to surrender to the mind, symbolized by the yellow bike. He rides the winding road of life, dressed in the appropriate protective gear for his journey. Victory can be achieved when physical and mental powers are maintained in balance. The Rider has conquered fear and now enjoys the unlimited possibilities of that freedom. His triumph is shown by his smile and raised hands. The Pleiades on his shirt, outside of himself, suggests he has not yet become aware of higher consciousness. The Key's number, 7 represents the analytical mind and the potential development of inner resources.

IN A READING: Be in charge of your own life. Don't let emotions, disadvantages, expectations, other people, or anything else dictate who you are. Take control and enjoy your triumph. Allow your conscious will to guide you. Travel is indicated, possibly a major move.

MEDITATION: I release fear and open my mind to unlimited possibilities.

DAILY READING: Today is a day to review your goals. Make sure they are actually yours and not imposed on you from something outside yourself.

KEY 8 FORTITUDE

Spiritual strength is the strongest force in the Universe.

PRIMARY CONCEPTS: Inner Strength, Spiritual Awareness, Confidence

DESCRIPTION: Key 8 shows a martial artist in a white uniform with a black belt. He is preparing to break boards. There are four boards set up on two concrete blocks. His eyes are closed. He stands on a blue matted floor. There is sunlight streaming in from the window in the background.

COMMENTARY: The martial artist is in a meditative pose, gathering the serenity and inner strength which comes from spirit. Self confidence is the by product of that connection. When you have no doubts, you can achieve anything. He knows physical strength alone is not enough to be successful. He wears white, the color of purity and truth. His black belt signifies maturity and completion in martial arts. The yellow boards, the color of the mind, are challenges to overcome. He stands on a blue foundation of peace and serenity, the acknowledgment of his inner strength. Sunlight represents spiritual awareness breaking through, illuminating the shadows of doubt. The Key's number, 8 indicates success, power, and material freedom.

IN A READING: This card represents spiritual strength overcoming disbelief. It may sound simple but there are often shadows of doubt lingering in your subconscious.

Time after time these fears produce failure. You must exorcise all of your uncertainty to harness this phenomenal strength. That is the true challenge.

MEDITATION: I am confident in my capability to achieve success.

DAILY READING: You have an unlimited supply of inner strength. Today is the day to demonstrate it.

KEY 9 GUIDANCE

The Universe provides an infinite supply of knowledge.

PRIMARY CONCEPTS: Seeker of Knowledge, Counsel

DESCRIPTION: Key 9 shows a student sitting at a study table in a large library. He is wearing a yellow shirt. Several reference books are on the table with a laptop computer, smart phone, and index cards. The tables are illuminated by gold and green lamps with merkaba shaped shades. Rows of bookshelves extend into the background. The floor is blue.

COMMENTARY: There is an infinite supply of wisdom in the Universe just waiting to be tapped into. Seeking knowledge and guidance is sometimes necessary. The best source of that counsel comes from within us. Our instincts and experience help us every day. It is never a sign of weakness to ask for help from the vast accumulated knowledge of our fellow travelers on this journey. That is why there is more than one of us here. The student is actively engaged in seeking information. His yellow shirt represents the intellectual process. The books and other tools are external resources while the merkaba lamps and blue floor indicate that inner wisdom is also present. The merkaba is a vehicle for transformation and so is knowledge. The open library design reflects his open mind. The Key's number, 9 is the number of pure intellect and of initiation, because it is the trinity of trinities. It also represents completion or the end of a cycle.

IN A READING: Be open to guidance. Do not limit your resources. The wisdom you seek can come from outside of yourself or within. It is always available. This card could also represent the need to share your knowledge with others.

MEDITATION: I am open to the guidance offered by the Universe.

DAILY READING: Today is the day to ask questions. You will never find the answers you seek if you do not ask.

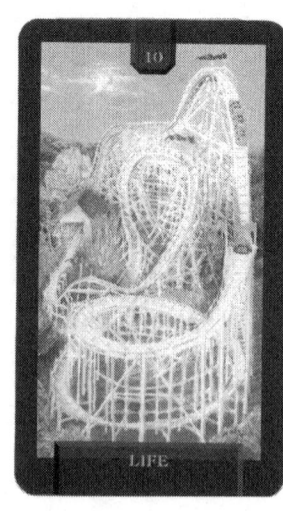

Key 10 Life

Changing perspective changes everything.

Primary Concepts: Destiny, Cycles, Perspective

Description: Key 10 depicts a large, white, lattice work roller coaster with many loops, turns, ups and downs. The four sets of pennants represent the elements; fire, water, air, and earth. Magical symbols for each of these elements are worked into the pattern of the lattice. The building is the starting and ending point for the ride. There are two occupied cars, one red and one yellow.

Commentary: The coaster accurately depicts the ups and downs of life, seemingly outside of our control. There are many times we cannot change what happens to us. Sometimes we are chugging uphill and everything seems fine and then life drops us so fast we feel totally out of control. This is just the way it is. We can't get off of the ride and have no power to stop it. Sometimes it is thrilling and sometimes it is terrifying. Our only power comes with our perspective, how we choose to view what happens to us and whether or not we accept it or resist it. Resistance causes much more pain. The building represents the point where one cycle ends and a new one begins. The riders cannot see the twists and turns ahead of them but from a higher perspective, the entire roller coaster is apparent.

IN A READING: A new cycle is beginning. Like every cycle, it will have positive and negative experiences. No matter what happens, you still have a choice in how you react. It is your perspective that makes the difference. Everything happens for a reason. Accept your destiny.

MEDITATION: I embrace life's challenges with grace.

DAILY READING: Take a look at your situation from a new perspective. Today is the day to accept what happens.

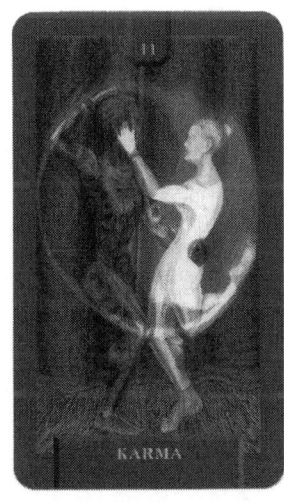

KEY 11 KARMA

The Universe is always just.

PRIMARY CONCEPTS: Justice, Cause/Effect, Yin/Yang

DESCRIPTION: Key 11 shows two dancers in a circular spotlight on a red curtained stage. The man is dressed in black and the woman wears white. The spotlight reflects the Yin/Yang symbol. Their bodies are posed to compliment the light. A wooden floor supports the couple.

COMMENTARY: The man and woman are polar opposites yet they complement each other perfectly. The position captured in the spotlight expresses the classic Yin/Yang, the ancient symbol of duality. Yin represents the negative energies and Yang the positive. While these energies have traditionally been associated with masculine and feminine forces, negative/black with the feminine and positive/white with the masculine, the image indicates that those forces are not gender based. Everything balances eventually. Karma is not a forced punishment but an opportunity to balance the positive and negative forces in the Universe. Positive is not necessarily good and negative is not necessarily bad. They are just two opposing forces. As we go through life we will experience both extremes and our challenge is to bring ourselves back to the center, to the stability of balance. The red curtain expresses the primal energy of the Universe. The wood floor represents strength and flexibility and the reliability of Karma.

IN A READING: True justice will prevail. The law of cause and effect does not discriminate. This card indicates a legal issue or a personal struggle. Justice here represents what is fair to all parties involved, not what any one person wants. Balance will occur.

MEDITATION: I trust in the Universe to dispense true justice.

DAILY READING: Recognize today that everything will equal out eventually. Let go of a need to get even.

KEY 12 CHOICE

There are always choices.

PRIMARY CONCEPTS: Decision, Suspension, Ripple Effect

DESCRIPTION: Key 12 shows the inside of a car. The view is from the driver's perspective, whose left hand is on the top of the steering wheel. Blue dashboard lights illuminate the interior. The car is in a freeway traffic jam approaching an exit off to the right. There is a green and white overhead sign saying "Quantum Exit Open."

COMMENTARY: Choice is what life is all about. We are constantly making decisions. The driver in the car has the option of staying in gridlock or taking an open exit which will lead in another direction. We can also choose to stay where we are, which could be a place of comfort and familiarity, or at any moment take another path. Signs will point out a new way. The only thing required is to notice these signs and act accordingly. The driver is obviously in control of the car. Blue lights in the interior indicate the spirituality underlying and illuminating every choice. Traffic gridlock symbolizes suspension of movement. "Quantum" on the green exit sign suggests even the smallest step can be a transformation. Every decision we make has a gradually spreading influence just like a pebble dropped in water creates endless ripples.

IN A READING: There are endless possibilities in life and if you are not content where you are, make a choice. It is time for a change. You can decide to stay where you are, but that is still a choice. The stagnation you are experiencing will continue.

MEDITATION: I will be open to the signs that point my way.

DAILY READING: Today is the day to decide. Take the steps necessary to transform your life.

KEY 13 TRANSITION

Change results in transformation.

PRIMARY CONCEPTS: Change, Passage, Transformation

DESCRIPTION: Key 13 depicts a golden colored suspension bridge. It is surrounded by clouds and there are green mountains in the background.

COMMENTARY: This card conveys the idea of moving from one place to another, or in other words, change. The bridge is painted gold symbolizing that there is a Divine force at work that instigates and oversees the passages in our lives. Changes happen. We can fight against them or we can recognize that all change is an exercise in growth for us and has the potential for transformation. We don't like the idea of change in our lives because we fear the unknown. Digging in our heels and resisting will not prevent it from occurring. The clouds obscure where the bridge leads, suggesting it is not about the destination. Green mountains ensure it is to a place of growth.

IN A READING: Change is coming as it always does, and it may be dramatic. The change may have already occurred and you are just now experiencing the effects, inside or outside of yourself. Embrace it and transform.

MEDITATION: I do not resist growth and the changes it brings.

DAILY READING: Transformation requires change. Release something today that is holding you back.

KEY 14 DISCERNMENT

When balanced and focused the path will become clear.

PRIMARY CONCEPTS: Equilibrium, Harmony, Balance

DESCRIPTION: Key 14 shows a costumed figure balancing on a tightrope. The costume is a white owl, including a mask with large eyes, feathered wings, and talons on her feet. Her left foot is on the golden rope. She is holding a balance bar which is half gold and half silver. The only light is on her, leaving the background in darkness.

COMMENTARY: It is difficult to make the choices that keep us in harmony. Discernment, which is selective judgment, should always be used. The acrobat stands on a rope representing her life path. The bar she holds signifies balance. Silver is the spiritual nature and gold the physical. She must keep these in perfect balance to continue her journey successfully. The owl costume suggests that wisdom is necessary to maintain equilibrium, with large eyes for focus, wings for spirituality, and talons to ground her to her path. She stands on one foot, preparing for her next step with the light illuminating her journey. Being human, we often overindulge, forget our spiritual lessons, react from emotional baggage, and pretty much make a mess of things. When we realize this we just need to get back on the rope and try again.

IN A READING: This card calls for thoughtful, wise choosing and good judgment. If you feel overwhelmed, remember to focus on the task at hand. Taking one step at a time is all that is necessary to bring yourself back into balance. With proper discernment the path will become clear. Spiritual guidance is always available.

MEDITATION: I focus my attention and energy on the present moment.

DAILY READING: Review your options today. Discern what is right for you and choose wisely.

Key 15 Materialism

Attachment to material things is a destructive illusion.

Primary Concepts: Illusion, Deception, Addiction

Description: Key 15 depicts a party inside a garish apartment. Well dressed people are milling around in various stages of inebriation. In the foreground the host sits on a chartreuse couch preparing drugs for his guests. He is wearing dark blue. A hand gun, a roll of money, prescription bottles, scales, and other drug paraphernalia are on the glass table. The woman on his right sits at his feet smiling up at him. She is dressed in gold. The man on his left is obviously passed out. He is dressed in faded blue. The floor is red brick.

Commentary: This card graphically expresses the danger of living only for materialistic gratification rather than balancing the material with spiritual fulfillment. The people are being deceived by the host and by artificial enjoyment and delusional pleasure, which could take away the very thing they are trying to enhance, their lives. The four elemental colors: red, blue, yellow, and green are present in the card but not in their pure form. Dark red in the brick floor is the wrong use of power. Faded blue indicates a weakened spiritual state. The blue suit of the host reflects his intuition, which he uses for manipulation. The dark yellow dress suggests the ego's control. Chartreuse indicates the mind's interference with growth. The transparent table holds the physical tools of the host's operation. What he offers is based on illusion. There is nothing wrong with material satisfaction, but as with everything there needs to be a balance. Society is addicted to the illusion of materialism, which places the value of life in a very precarious position and alone will never provide true fulfillment.

IN A READING: Be very careful. You could be deceiving yourself or someone else could be taking advantage of you. What you are seeing might be an illusion. This card could also indicate an addiction is influencing the situation. Value is placed on the gratification achieved through material attainment and the ego rather than spiritual fulfillment.

MEDITATION: I am no longer afraid to look beyond my illusions.

DAILY READING: Deception surrounds this day. Be aware of your interactions. Do not take someone's word at face value.

KEY 16 INTERVENTION

Enlightenment can be shocking.

PRIMARY CONCEPTS: Disruption, Enlightenment

DESCRIPTION: Key 16 shows a family fleeing in obvious terror after a large tree has just fallen on their house. Although the family does not appear to be hurt, the house has sustained considerable damage. It is a two story house. The tree was standing in the front yard of the home and the broken, jagged stump is in the foreground. The family, a mother, father, two children, and a dog escape down the stone front walk. He is wearing red and she is wearing blue.

COMMENTARY: This card is a reminder that when something happens to us seemingly outside of our control, we still have choices. It is a turning point. We can choose to deny our fate and rant about how unfair it is or we can accept what has happened, and choose to take an active stance toward resolving the issue. We can search for an answer and begin a plan to go on with our lives. It is an opportunity to analyze what we are learning from our experience. Perhaps this family will learn there are many people willing to help them or how fortunate they are to just have each other safe and sound. Maybe they will move to a new neighborhood where they will make lasting friendships or use this opportunity to remodel their home. The possibilities are endless once you stop wasting energy wishing things were different. It is sad and scary to go through a disruptive experience, but we are here to learn to conquer these fears. When we accept life altering experiences and do what needs to be done, we become stronger. The man and woman in red and blue clothing represent physical and emotional reactions and the children and dog are responsibilities we all carry. The stone path signifies no matter what the circumstances, there is always a way. Not all breaks are clean, as the jagged stump suggests. Sometimes there is much to deal with.

IN A READING: This card represents an abrupt awakening, usually from unforeseen circumstances. It may alter everything you believe. You have control over how you react. It is an opportunity for enlightenment.

MEDITATION: I see life's challenges as opportunities.

DAILY READING: Disruption is possible today. Choose to view challenges from an enlightened perspective.

KEY 17 MEDITATION

Deep in silence the subconscious speaks.

PRIMARY CONCEPTS: Insight, Inspiration, Higher Self

DESCRIPTION: Key 17 shows a young woman who is meditating. She is sitting in a traditional meditative posture with a look of serenity. Her fingers are positioned in a meditation mudra with her thumbs and forefingers touching. She wears purple and is sitting on a purple cushion with gold trim and tassels. The floor beneath her is hardwood and there is white furniture in the background. The blue sky is visible through the skylight above her.

COMMENTARY: Meditation quiets the mind and unleashes creative power. It has numerous health benefits and spiritual value. This card says meditation should be a way of life. It is connecting with our higher selves to seek answers to all of life's mysteries. We are constantly asking questions, but don't always listen for the answers. Meditation offers the opportunity to listen and the answers are there. A mudra is a spiritual hand gesture. The position of her fingers is believed to help instill wisdom and enlightenment. Purple signifies her desire to master this ancient art. Gold, the color of spirituality suggests her link to the Divine. The hardwood floor supports and grounds her while the open room design reflects her open mind.

IN A READING: Look within for answers and insights. Use meditation to connect with your higher self for inspiration, inner calm and peace. This card assures all will be well.

MEDITATION: I still my mind and open to the infinite universe.

DAILY READING: Do something today that inspires you: walk in the park, listen to music, or get a massage.

KEY 18 INTUITION

The answers are within.

PRIMARY CONCEPTS: Perception, Imagination, Reflection

DESCRIPTION: Key 18 depicts a woman reading a crystal ball. The only light in the room comes from the illuminated ball. Her hands are on either side of it. She wears a purple blouse and gold hoop earrings. The table is also purple.

COMMENTARY: Intuition comes from within. The reader is in a state of reflection. The crystal ball is just a tool to focus her perceptions and release her imagination. This card expresses the connection to the subconscious mind and the vast storehouse of knowledge available. It encourages the creative use of the imagination to find answers. Trusting feelings and listening to instincts are foreign to many people. They seek out authorities or research online for answers. Everyone has the ability to tap into this endless resource of information and guidance. The more it is used, the stronger it gets. The illuminated ball reflects the light within which she embraces. Purple is the color of imagination and mastery. She wears gold hoops in her ears. The circle is a symbol of infinity indicating the energy she connects with is never ending.

IN A READING: Trust your feelings. You have the ability to perceive the answers you seek. Reflection is necessary to engage your creativity and imagination. Be open to information from dreams. Do what feels right.

MEDITATION: I trust my own perceptions.

DAILY READING: If it feels wrong, it probably is. Act accordingly today.

Key 19 Illumination

Releasing limitations liberates the spirit.

Primary Concepts: Liberation, Joy, Freedom

Description: Key 19 shows a bareback rider and his white horse galloping along the beach in the sunshine. The rider's dark hair is flowing behind him. He is barefoot and shirtless.

Commentary: This card is all about lack of restrictions. There are no restraints on the rider or the horse as they enjoy the ride. The masculine energy of the sun and the rider express the strength freedom provides. This energy empowers. White is the color of cleansing, the release of limitation. The rider has control over his past restrictions. They do not control him. True joy is the liberation of the spirit.

In a Reading: Enjoy your freedom. Revel in the healing power of the sun. A period of joy and liberation is at hand. Use this positive energy for empowerment. You are in control.

Meditation: I release limitation and embrace freedom.

Daily Reading: Today is surrounded by positive energy. Use it to your advantage.

Key 20 Awareness

Awareness is necessary to perceive truth.

Primary Concepts: Spiritual Awakening, Renewal, Consciousness

Description: Key 20 depicts a nighttime block party or outdoor concert. There is a band playing from a stage. Many people are enjoying the entertainment. Their attention is focused on the performance. One woman stands out. She has noticed a shooting star soaring through the night sky. Her gold colored shirt is illuminated.

Commentary: We often miss signs and symbols from the universe as we go through our busy days. We are focused on what we have to do and where we have to go, on our problems and concerns. This card says if we pay attention, if we are aware, the universe will offer us guidance and assistance. We seldom notice the beauty of a hawk soaring across the sky, the synchronicity of all the traffic lights turning green for us, the love that passes between a parent and child at the park. These gifts, like the shooting star remind us to be conscious of our surroundings for spiritual upliftment and renewal. We don't have to search for what we're looking for; if we are aware, it is always there. The woman wears gold, a color that reflects spiritual energy and awakening to one's own power.

In a Reading: What you are looking for is already there. This card represents a spiritual awakening. Consciousness has been raised and there's no going back. This will allow you to see the world differently. Within this new awareness your answers will become apparent.

MEDITATION: I am aware.

DAILY READING: Today it is important to be conscious of your surroundings. This awareness will lead to a new discovery.

KEY 21 COMPLETION

Every ending is a new beginning.

PRIMARY CONCEPTS: Integration, Completed Cycle, Mastery, Success

DESCRIPTION: Key 21 shows the student from Key 0 Beginning teaching the Tarot to others. She is facing a group of people, seated at a large wooden table. The purple layout cloth, first seen in Key 2 Wisdom is on the table illustrating the Seven Card Merkaba Spread. She is explaining the spread through the information on the white board. Her blouse is purple. The walls and carpet of the room are green. She holds the cards in her right hand and points to the board with her left.

COMMENTARY: The student has become the teacher. This cycle is successfully completed. She has come a long way from opening her first deck and after years of study and reading the cards she is ready to share what she has learned. The end of a cycle is not just about endings. We also have opportunities to share what we have learned along the way whether we know it or not. We may not formally teach a class, but family members, friends and even complete strangers learn from our example. Our experiences help others going through something similar, to lessen someone else's burden just a little or guide them down an easier path. We are all connected and every cycle is integrated into the whole. She wears the color of mastery. Earth tones surround her representing her growth in this cycle. Her receptive hand is raised toward the wisdom of the Tarot. Her giving hand holds her deck. The merkaba is a vehicle of enlightenment and integration. The teacher has integrated information about the Tarot and now enlightens others.

IN A READING: This card suggests the successful completion of a cycle. Celebrate your achievement. Soon a new cycle will begin. Integrate what you have learned into your life and let go of what is no longer needed. Share your experience with others.

MEDITATION: I am a positive influence on the world.

DAILY READING: Someone around you needs what you already know. Share yourself today.

Introduction to the Elements

Introduction to the Elements

It is believed that everything in the universe contains four basic elements: fire, water, air, and earth. These elements exist in both physical and non-physical forms. The physical aspects of the elements are easy to see and understand. We feel the firmness of the earth beneath us, the air we breathe sustains us. The non-physical aspects are just as important to comprehend. What makes us who we are is much more than just a physical body. Our thoughts, emotions, beliefs, and ideas are all forms of energy that may become manifest within our physical world, but do not solely reside there. Likewise other energies completely outside of conscious awareness have a profound effect on us mentally, physically, emotionally, and spiritually.

It is the creative energies of the four elements that have manifested our world and everything within it. They are dependent on one another to survive. Without air, a flame will perish. It is our day to day struggle to bring these energies into balance that defines our existence. It is that struggle, with its highs and lows, positives and negatives that is depicted within the Element cards of Today's Journey Tarot.

The Elements are comprised of four suits; Fire, Water, Air, and Earth. Each suit is numbered from One to Ten and includes a family unit of Child, Youth, Mother, and Father.

FIRE

Fire is symbolized by the color red. Each of the Fire cards is surrounded by a red border. They are associated with the direction south and the season of summer, both denoting its warmth. Fire always reaches up as if it wants or needs to exceed itself. If not checked, its creative passion can easily become uncontrolled.

The fire cards depict dynamic leaders of industry who create and draw success with the power of their own will. They correspond with the suit of Wands and represent energy, strength, authority and ambition. If not balanced, fire's ambition can become too competitive, blocking sense and reason which is a heavy burden difficult to carry. Fire's passion can give the strength to achieve anything desired. That same passion can burn out of control.

WATER

Water is symbolized by the color blue. Each of the Water cards is framed by a blue border. It is associated with the direction of west and the season autumn, the time of harvest. The nature of water is elusive. It is difficult to prevent its natural flow. On the surface a river may seem to be gently flowing along while deep below turbulent undercurrents are moving with violent intensity. Because of this characteristic water is associated with our subconscious and emotional aspects. The human body is composed of more than ninety percent water. It may benefit us to pay closer attention to this part of our being. Water sustains us, showing us its healing qualities. It represents all emotions. It washes and cleanses. It can be determined, even stubborn. Rain will eventually dissolve even the largest stone.

Within the water cards, which correspond to the suit of Cups, we find those who celebrate life, and friends and lovers who follow their instincts and move with the flow of the universe. Some resist that flow, holding on to emotional pain, rather than releasing it.

AIR

Air is symbolized by the color yellow and has corresponding yellow borders. Its direction is east where the sun rises each day and its season is spring, both symbolizing its sense of renewal. Air is vital to our survival yet is seldom seen or heard. Its influence can be physical but most often it is beneath the surface of our awareness. Air rules the mind, the intellect, abstract thought, and knowledge. It can be uplifting like a kite held aloft by cheerfulness and optimism or it can be destructive like a devastating tornado. Using thought alone without feeling is building a house without a foundation. A strong enough wind will blow it away.

Within the Air cards, which correspond to the suit of Swords, we find a variety of thinkers. Some use the knowledge they have gained for their own benefit, and others find themselves trapped by thought, unable to feel. There are students and teachers of rationality, thought, justice, movement, independence, cleverness, clarity, and truth. They teach the triumphs and tragedies of the mind.

EARTH

Earth cards can be identified by their green borders. Its direction is north and its season winter. These both represent a lack of light, like the safety and security of the womb. The Earth is our home. It is our source of solidity and stability and the largest physical manifestation of the material world. It rotates as it moves through the universe showing us all things move in cycles.

The Earth cards, which correspond to the suit of Pentacles, represent growth, stability, abundance, patience, strength, and endurance. Focusing solely on the physical can manifest great abundance. That victory would be hollow without thought or emotion. Patience can easily turn to stagnation. To give without emotion and create without thought is to ignore what the earth most wants to teach; find balance and experience true stability.

FAMILY UNIT

Within each of the four Elements there is a family unit of Child, Youth, Mother, and Father. They correspond to the court cards of Page, Knight, Queen, and King.

The Child represents the Element expressed in its infancy. It is the awakening of the attributes of the Element. These cards often represent children who embody these qualities.

The Youth personifies the energy of adolescence within each Element. It is the expression of passion, emotion, thought and devotion before it has the opportunity to mature. These cards often represent young people or people expressing immaturity.

The Mother characterizes the matured Element in the reflective nature of the feminine. Her character is influenced by the subconscious, intuitive and emotional psyche.

The Father characterizes the matured element in the active nature of the masculine. His character is influenced by the conscious, logical and physical psyche.

Fire

One of Fire

Passion can be a guide like a star on the horizon or it can consume like a fire.

Primary Concepts: Passion, Energy, Power

Description: The One of Fire shows the glowing Sun in brilliant colors of yellow, orange, and red. Solar flares shoot out into the darkness of space.

Commentary: The Sun sustains life on Earth. Without its fire we would not exist. When we harness this strength we can accomplish anything. Its passion creates unimaginable beauty. When we channel its energy we can realize our dreams.

In a Reading: All of the Ones can signify new beginnings. For this card that beginning is imbued with the Element of Fire and all of the qualities it represents. It is the ultimate essence of the Fire. This powerful new cycle is driven by creativity and passion, or the strength to harness or utilize this force.

Meditation: I am sustained by the driving force of the Sun.

Daily Reading: Tap into the unlimited energy of Fire available today. Let your passion guide you.

Two of Fire

Hope is a light that dispels the shadows of doubt.

Primary Concepts: New Enterprise, Hope for Success

Description: The Two of Fire shows a ribbon cutting ceremony for a new lighting business. The merchant stands beneath the stone arch of the strip mall and holds oversized scissors to cut the red ribbon. News reporters and the mayor cheer him on. The name of the store, Kamin Lighting, is written in dark red on the window. Several of the lighting fixtures visible within the store are found in other cards.

Commentary: This card expresses that moment when all of the hard work, planning, and dreaming is finally realized and desires have become a reality. The store owner is proud of what he has accomplished and is looking forward to the success of his new business. There is still work to be done as he begins the day to day operations, but this milestone is an indicator of greater things he can achieve. The ribbon cutting ceremony signifies the store is now open for business. Large scissors cut away the merchant's doubts of his dream being fulfilled. The arch is the threshold to his future. Kamin is a German word related to fire.

In a Reading: This card reassures you that you have arrived at a place of reward for all the effort you have put forth. If you can keep the momentum alive with a positive outlook there is no limit to where you can go from here. This is just the beginning. Have hope for the future.

MEDITATION: I release doubt and embrace hope for success.

DAILY READING: Celebrate your progress today. Be proud of what you have accomplished.

THREE OF FIRE

Dedication turns dreams into reality.

PRIMARY CONCEPTS: Realization, Success in Business

DESCRIPTION: The Three of Fire depicts the successful lighting store business from the previous card. It is filled with merchandise and smiling employees. The gold door handle is prominently displayed beside the front window. The merchant is sitting at a red topped desk with a customer. The lights are all lit and the store is very bright. The sign above the employees reads, "Home and Business Solutions."

COMMENTARY: The store has progressed to a prosperous business. This card expresses the realization of a goal. The ribbon cutting ceremony from the Two of Fire celebrated the opening of the store. Hard work and dedication has turned the dream into an ongoing reality. Gold indicates coming into one's own power. The illuminated interior reflects spiritual support for the merchant's passion. While the card emphasizes business, the sign above the employees suggests passion can be channeled for any endeavor.

IN A READING: Success is realized. The commitment to a business or any other undertaking is fulfilled. Hard work pays off. When you follow your passion, you are working in harmony with the universe. Unseen influences will support your goal with coincidences and opportunities.

MEDITATION: My dreams are realized.

DAILY READING: Be open to unseen influences today. Synchronicities point the way to success.

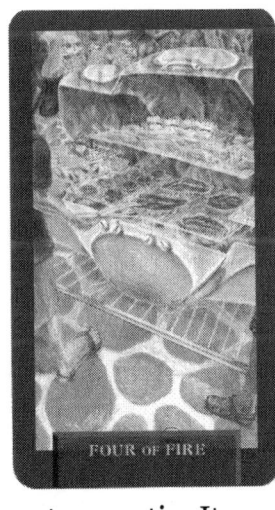

FOUR OF FIRE

Celebrate abundance.

PRIMARY ASPECTS: Celebration, Abundance, Prosperity

DESCRIPTION: The Four of Fire shows a backyard barbeque with a grill laden with food. There are people milling around enjoying themselves. The white grill stands on a stone patio. Its embers are red hot. Smoke and steam rise from the fire.

COMMENTARY: This card's simple message is to enjoy life. It reminds us to take time out of our busy schedules to celebrate the prosperity we have been given. The bounty of food represents the manifestation of abundance. The intense focus of the flame cooks the food like our focus creates the world we live in. The white grill indicates it is a spiritual process. Smoke symbolizes the desire for abundance rising into the ethers. The stones represent material manifestation in the physical world. An attitude of celebration is essential to attract positive results.

IN A READING: Prosperity and good times are here or on their way. There may be a cause for celebration coming soon and it should be recognized. Enjoy. Acknowledge the abundance that surrounds you in whatever form it may take.

MEDITATION: I celebrate my abundance and the prosperity that is to come.

DAILY READING: Take a moment today to give thanks for everything you have.

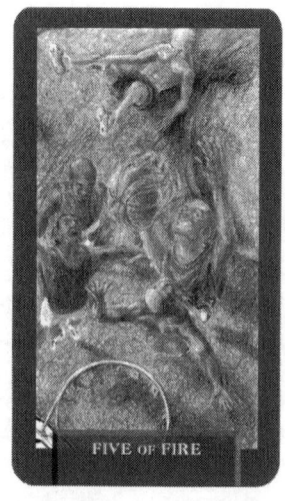

FIVE OF FIRE

Life can be confusing and chaotic.

PRIMARY CONCEPTS: Confusion, Inner Turmoil, Chaos, Competition

DESCRIPTION: The Five of Fire shows a group of young men playing basketball. No teams are evident. They are all dressed in varying shades of red. The competition has gotten out of control. One person has fallen. The players have intense, angry looks on their faces as they scramble for the ball.

COMMENTARY: Each man is playing only for himself. Their faces show determination to win at any cost. Their energy is chaotic and may even be destructive. In our multitasking world today we often allow our energies to deplete to the point of exhaustion. We go at such a pace that we become careless and could hurt ourselves or others. Unfortunately many people end up unable to see the consequences or selfishness of their actions. Road rage is one example of this type of energy out of control. Even hurtful words or neglected relationships can be a result of the turmoil in our lives or in our minds. Red, the predominant color, symbolizes the intensity of the players' energy which they are uselessly discarding.

IN A READING: This card is telling you to be in command of your own power. Be conscious of energy that is out of control and do something to refocus. It is time to calm down and prioritize. Get a grip and use your energy in productive ways.

MEDITATION: I unite with inner peace and it becomes my reality.

DAILY READING: Calm down. Refocus and release your need to win.

Six of Fire

Leadership comes in many types of roles.

Primary Concepts: Leadership, Victory, Triumph

Description: The Six of Fire depicts an athlete carrying a lighted torch. She is running down a city street with a crowd of well wishers and reporters cheering her on. The silver torch is in her right hand and she wears red and white.

Commentary: This is a moment of triumph and victory. The torchbearer has earned this honor through her many successes. She is deservedly proud and confident, a symbol of the best of the human spirit. Others look up to her. Their admiration elevates her from the role of athlete to leader. Anyone who becomes accomplished in their field may have to face the responsibility of leadership. A leader knows that individual success is something to be proud of but true victory contributes to the well being of all. The silver torch is a symbol of victory that lights the way for others. Red signifies her passion to succeed and white, her purity of heart.

In a Reading: This card represents triumph. It has already occurred or is about to occur. Something proposed will be successful. Others look to you for direction or you may be offered a position of leadership. Victory is assured.

Meditation: I am proud of my accomplishments.

Daily Reading: Opportunities presented today will be successful. Celebrate your victory.

Seven of Fire

Don't give in to the pressures of life.

Primary Concepts: Pressure, Adversity, Overcoming Challenges

Description: The Seven of Fire shows a celebrity walking the red carpet. The paparazzi are lined behind the ropes with microphones and the flashes of their cameras go off as he passes. He is all smiles and gives them a thumbs up with his right hand while waving to them with his left. The celebrity wears a black suit and red tie. Behind him the doors are still open on his black limousine.

Commentary: We get exactly what we ask for. The celebrity has reached a level of fame that brings with it the expectation of a lack of privacy. There are times when that may be uncomfortable or even overwhelming but it goes along with his chosen career. Everything in life has benefits and times of adversity. If we give into the pressure we may lose what we have struggled to obtain. His smile does not tell the whole story. It is a continuous effort to maintain his position of notoriety. The lights blind him. He can't even see where he's going. All of his body language is a mask he wears to hide the pressure and display what everyone else wants to see. The red reflects the tremendous amount of energy it takes to keep up the façade. His black clothes and car represent the only insulation from the daily onslaught. Black is a color of protection.

IN A READING: You have to accept the demands that go with any choice you make. This card suggests that you are struggling with pressures and it is time to choose whether or not what you want is worth it. Adversity comes with any situation and can be a catalyst for failure if not overcome.

MEDITATION: I overcome adversity to get what I desire.

DAILY READING: Don't give in to pressure today. If you are doing what you want, persevere.

Eight of Fire

Energy is always moving.

PRIMARY CONCEPTS: Energy, Movement

DESCRIPTION: The Eight of Fire shows a night sky filled with fireworks. The intensity of the reds, purples, and yellows suggests a very large display.

COMMENTARY: Fireworks are beautiful. They express a massive level of energy without being destructive. It is the energy itself that draws the crowds. To see such power controlled and channeled into a spectacle of light enthralls and delights us. It takes a tremendous amount of effort, organization, planning, and precision to control this force. One mistake could destroy the whole show. We believe it is something beyond our capabilities. The fireworks symbolize the powerful movement of energy.

IN A READING: This card suggests that you too can exert this control. By focusing your attention, you have power over your own energy, which is boundless. You can use it in many different ways, some are positive and creative like the fireworks and some are as destructive as an atomic bomb. It is up to you to gather your energy and channel it in a way that gives you as much pleasure as a million lights in the night sky.

MEDITATION: I am in control of my own energy.

DAILY READING: Use energy wisely today. Do not allow it to become so intense it burns out. Take control.

NINE OF FIRE

Do not trade liberty for security.

PRIMARY CONCEPTS: Security, Isolation, Protection

DESCRIPTION: The Nine of Fire depicts the front entrance of a gated community. The closed gate is black wrought iron. There is a keyless entry pad on the gate post. The drive is leading to houses seen in the distance. They are yellow and red.

COMMENTARY: This card expresses the fine line between security and isolation. A gated community offers safety for its residents. No one can get in unless they have the security code, limiting access to a select group. A certain amount of security is necessary for our protection, but we can withdraw into that sense of safety and find ourselves isolated from the world. The fire forged metal gate indicates cold, subdued passion. Its bars could become a prison. Black is the color of protection. Yellow and red indicate the mind's energy contained by fear.

IN A READING: While you may need to do what is necessary for your security, be careful not to limit yourself in the process. Do not isolate yourself in your search for safety.

MEDITATION: I am secure within myself.

DAILY READING: Do not isolate yourself today. Spend time with others.

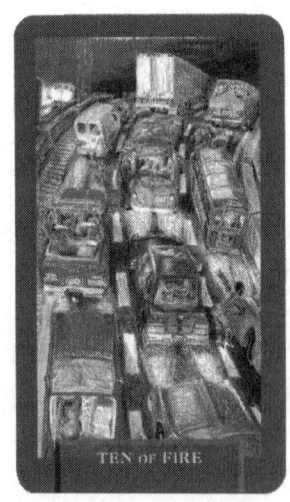

TEN OF FIRE

Frustration without hope leads to anger.

PRIMARY CONCEPTS: Burdened, Overwhelmed, Frustrated

DESCRIPTION: The Ten of Fire shows a traffic jam on a three lane freeway. It has obviously been going on for a while because people are outside of their vehicles and most are exhibiting frustration and anger at the delay. There is a wide variety of vehicles caught in the traffic jam: a semi truck, school bus, convertible, passenger vehicles, and a van. The cause of the problem is not apparent because of a hill immediately ahead of them. The sun is setting with a reddish glow.

COMMENTARY: We can all relate to the aggravation and frustration of being stuck in traffic. It happens all the time. We may sit for long periods and are blind to what is going on ahead of us or how long the delay will be. There are times in life when things happen that impede our progress and we feel at a standstill. Often we don't know the reason and are overwhelmed and feel resentment for something that is beyond our control. Frustration does not make the burden easier. It can lead to anger and agitation. We must remember that these delays are only temporary. In time the traffic clears and we move on our way. The same is true for life. Everything passes eventually and we can move forward. Bad times are replaced by good times. The variety of vehicles suggests this happens to everyone at one time or another. The red sky symbolizes the intense energy that could lead to an explosive situation.

IN A READING: You feel like you are not making progress. Something outside of your control is not allowing you to move forward. Don't give up. Try to ride it out or seek positive solutions. Right now you are overwhelmed and can't see the answer, but in time it will come.

MEDITATION: I do not give in to frustration.

DAILY READING: Today is not a day for action. Something may be in your way that you are not seeing. Wait for it to clear.

Child of Fire

Misdirected passion can lead to obsession.

Primary Concepts: Immature passion, Obsession, Potential

Description: The Child of Fire shows a boy sitting cross-legged on the floor with his back against a big overstuffed orange couch. He is mesmerized in front of a TV screen playing a video game. Images from the screen are reflected in the room: on the floor, the couch, and even the boy. Sunlight shines through a window behind him. The floor is green and yellow. There are wooden beams across a blue ceiling.

Commentary: This card demonstrates what can happen when we become obsessed with anything. Our focus and energy are out of balance and we miss other opportunities. The Child of Fire is very passionate about his games. He plays them for hours on end excluding everything else from his life. This kind of obsession can affect relationships, jobs, and even health. It is an immature use of passion and drive. If that same energy was focused on a productive endeavor, imagine what he could accomplish. The potential would be endless. Orange is the color of sociability, which he has turned his back on. The reflected images from the game are becoming his reality. Sunshine streams in the window behind him offering an alternative, but his entire focus is on the artificial light from the screen. The coloring on the floor is not even or balanced suggesting the mind's influence impeding growth. Heavy beams hang over his head. They are the weight of his obsession.

IN A READING: This card could represent a person (male or female) or a situation. This person has the energy and passion to accomplish anything. Attention and focus may be misdirected because of immaturity. He could easily become obsessive. This card could also represent a situation where there is a need to reevaluate where your energy is going. Don't waste it on obsessive pursuits especially if they are unproductive. Video games and everything else in life has a place but it is not meant to replace life itself.

MEDITATION: I do not waste my energy unproductively.

DAILY READING: With the proper focus you can accomplish anything today.

YOUTH OF FIRE

There is a difference between spontaneity and recklessness.

PRIMARY CONCEPTS: Raw Passion, Impulsive

DESCRIPTION: The Youth of Fire shows a young man roaring down a country highway on his motorcycle. He wears no protective gear as he rides along, just sunglasses. His bike, shirt, and hair are red. The bike is embossed with flames. He passes by a large field of cotton.

COMMENTARY: The raw passion of youth is a force that can sometimes be lost as we mature. The Youth of Fire takes risks and does what he wants without fear of losing control or caring what anyone else thinks. Passion out of control can be a dangerous thing but when directed can be creative and spontaneous. With awareness we are able to discern the difference. His lack of protective gear demonstrates his confidence and daring. The sunglasses reflect where he is right now. He does not see beyond that moment. Red symbolizes the intensity of his energy. The flames remind us that raw power can be destructive. The prosperous cotton field he passes represents the patience and controlled passion necessary for successful growth. The Youth does not see it.

IN A READING: This card could represent a person (male or female) or a situation. The person is impulsive and reckless. His passion is not responsibly directed. In a situation this card says to be careful and mindful about what you are doing. It reminds you not to use your energy in reckless pursuits. Stop and think before making any decision. It may also call for a need to be impulsive and take some controlled risks, just to keep things interesting.

MEDITATION: I am inspired to take chances.

DAILY READING: You might not be seeing clearly what you are creating in your life. Reevaluate where you are going.

MOTHER OF FIRE

Strength is needed for victory.

PRIMARY CONCEPTS: Creates Success, Strength, Mature Passion

DESCRIPTION: The Mother of Fire depicts a politician at an outdoor political rally. She waves to the crowd of well wishers on her way to the podium. She wears a red suit. The city skyline is behind her. A body guard stands off stage.

COMMENTARY: This card shows a woman who is passionate about life and goes after what she wants. She has all the characteristics needed to be a successful leader. She is strong and confident and works to create her own success and does not shy away from responsibility. This level of strength and mature passion is necessary to achieve her goals. It is not easy to campaign day after day but it is essential to be elected to office. She stands above the crowd in a red suit symbolizing strength. The city behind her offers innumerable opportunities and its skyscrapers suggest there are no limits to how high she can go. The guard represents her confidence and security.

IN A READING: This card could represent a person (male or female) or a situation. The person is a strong leader driven by her passion for success. She is confident, dynamic and outgoing. Whatever her attention is focused on has her full commitment. The card could also represent a situation where you have to be willing to give that level of commitment to achieve your goals. You create your own success. Strength and passion are needed for victory.

MEDITATION: I am confident in my ability to succeed.

DAILY READING: Commit to your own success today. Exert your strength.

FATHER OF FIRE

Focused passion attracts success.

PRIMARY CONCEPTS: Attracts Success, Focused Passion, Power

DESCRIPTION: The Father of Fire shows a successful businessman in his affluent office. He is on the top floor of a skyscraper busy making deals on the phone. His large desk resembles bare wood. The computer keyboard is part of the desk. The images on the monitor are clubs, equivalent to the Wands suit in the classic Tarot. There is a red picture on the back wall of a solitary tree. A floor to ceiling window occupies one wall of his office.

COMMENTARY: This card demonstrates the success and power that comes from focusing your passion and the consequences that accomplishment can bring. The Father of Fire has worked very hard for what he has. He has attracted his success with his dynamic personality and intense focus. All of his energy and time went into his business, while he neglected other areas of his life. He is isolated at the top. If he has not cultivated personal relationships or other interests along the way it can be a very lonely and unfulfilling position, as the picture on the wall suggests. The desk absorbs the keyboard just as the Father is totally immersed in his work. The window offers a distorted view of the world through the sheer curtains.

IN A READING: This card could represent a person (male or female) or a situation. The person is a dynamic and powerful leader who attracts success. He may be indifferent to personal relationships because of his focus on work. If this card represents a situation, it indicates success, especially in business. Always remember to keep your life in balance. Do not forfeit everything else while you are focused on a goal. Leadership is indicated.

MEDITATION: I attract success.

DAILY READING: There is a lot of successful energy around this day. It is your choice how to use it. Don't burn out.

Water

One of Water

Emotions can be tranquil like a still pond or violent like a storm at sea.

Primary Concepts: Deep Emotion, Unconditional Love

Description: The One of Water depicts the sea in all of its many forms, from smooth and calm to rough and stormy. On the left side a cloud with rain enters the card. On the right the sky is clear. The card is filled with various shades of blue.

Commentary: This card captures the complexity of emotions. They can be all over the place. Water is the element of emotion and the blue of this card suggests an abundance of love and healing. It nourishes all life. When conditions change and emotions shift, we can be filled with despair.

In a Reading: The One of Water can describe any kind of emotional challenge or represent the greatest love of all, unconditional love, in your life. It can also represent the beginning of a spiritual quest or awakening of a deep and abiding love.

Meditation: I maintain emotional balance in my life.

Daily Reading: Emotions are running high today. Stay in control.

Two of Water

A successful partnership enhances life.

Primary Concepts: Love, Partnership, Commitment

Description: The Two of Water shows a young couple gazing lovingly at each other as they walk hand in hand along the shallow water of the ocean. A full moon shines down upon the lovers. They both wear blue.

Commentary: This card depicts the fulfillment of a successful partnership. Whether that partnership is love, friendship, business, or anything else, choosing a partner should be done with great care. Too often we find ourselves attached to someone we barely know, can't trust, doesn't inspire us, or even abuses us in some way. A partner should be someone who enhances our life. The full moon and the predominant blue color reinforce the emotional commitment. They stand in the water suggesting their relationship is their foundation.

In a Reading: This card represents the forming of a new beneficial partnership or recommitment to an existing one. Do not settle for anything less than someone who enhances your life. Choose wisely and there is no limit to what you can achieve together.

Meditation: My relationships enhance my life.

Daily Reading: Positive energy surrounds relationships today. Give and receive love freely.

Three of Water

Friendship should be celebrated.

Primary Concepts: Celebration of Self, Friendship

Description: The Three of Water shows three young women enjoying time out together. They are sitting in the bar area of a busy restaurant. There is a blue candle in the center of the round table. The décor is mostly wood with large open design windows.

Commentary: Three women have met at a restaurant just to enjoy being together. They are preparing to toast one another. This card is about going out with friends and doing something fun. Friendship should be celebrated. The blue candle symbolizes their emotional freedom with one another. In this setting they are all equals, as the round table suggests. The wood décor emphasizes the strength and stability of their friendship. Their openness with each other is demonstrated by the design of the restaurant.

In a Reading: It is time to let your hair down and do something fun with people you enjoy being with. There could be a reason for a celebration, or you can celebrate just being together. Life is hectic and in order to stay in balance it is essential you make time for the people you enjoy. There may be a need to appreciate the person you are and what you have to give to others. This card could also indicate too much celebration. Don't overdo it.

MEDITATION: I celebrate and appreciate who I am.

DAILY READING: Today is a day to have fun doing what you want to do with the people you want to be with.

FOUR OF WATER

Life offers continuous opportunities.

PRIMARY CONCEPTS: Opportunity Missed, Opportunity Offered

DESCRIPTION: The Four of Water depicts a young man walking down a crowded urban street at night. He wears ear buds, green cargo pants, and a blue t-shirt. It has just rained and the reflection of the water illuminates him as it flows into a drain on the curb. There are people enjoying the evening at outdoor cafes and they beckon to him as he passes.

COMMENTARY: The self absorbed young man doesn't see or hear anything around him. He is plugged into his ear buds and looking down as his sandals splash through the puddles. This card accurately shows how many of us go through life. We bemoan our lack of opportunities while not paying attention to what is going on around us. We may recognize favorable circumstances when they are large enough to get our attention, such as a new job offer. It is the constant stream of opportunities always available that we miss. We go through our lives with blinders on, not paying attention to the little details. Any one of these could grow into a chance to make changes in our lives. The green and blue clothes suggest an abundance of emotional balance available to him. He splashes through his emotions as if they aren't there as the water disappears down the drain.

IN A READING: It is important to pay attention. Look for the signs the Universe is always sending your way that point you in new directions or answer your questions. This card is saying to open up your eyes, ears, and heart to the offerings of the Universe. The more you do this, the more you will recognize the synchronicities that lead you in the right direction. This skill must be practiced because a great deal of life is spent shutting out the world and its abundant gifts.

MEDITATION: I am open to the opportunities the Universe provides.

DAILY READING: Something you experience today leads to an offer. Pay attention.

Five of Water

It is impossible to move forward while looking back.

Primary Concepts: Regret, Disappointment, Attachment

Description: The Five of Water shows a middle aged man looking through his old high school yearbook. He is a former star athlete whose glory days are memorialized in the display behind him. There is a blue pennant on the wall that says Dolphins. His letterman's sweater sits framed next to gold and silver trophies. There is a glass with only ice left in it on the desk in front of him. He has a look of sadness and regret on his face.

Commentary: If we have a huge success early in life it is sometimes hard to top it and we long for those better times. We reminisce and revisit over and over again and wish we could go back. This is of course living in the past. We may believe it was better then, but that belief limits our possibilities for today. Our energy and attention goes to what has already occurred instead of what we could make of our lives now. It may be that we can never have exactly what we did before but the infinite possibilities in the Universe could even give us more. Besides, the past may not have been as good as we remember it. The man's shrine to the past shows where his focus is. He should learn from the mascot of his youth. Dolphins never swim backward. Like the ice in his glass, he is frozen in time.

IN A READING: Let go of the emotional attachment to the past and move forward. Build now for the future using what you've learned from the past, which is the way it is suppose to be. Regret and disappointment inhibit our ability to learn from the past. Release them.

MEDITATION: I release my attachment to the past and live for today.

DAILY READING: There is a future and it is time to start moving toward it. Start a new chapter today and don't look back.

SIX OF WATER

Innocence makes every experience a new discovery.

PRIMARY CONCEPTS: Sharing, Innocence, Childhood

DESCRIPTION: The Six of Water shows two little boys standing barefoot in a shallow creek. They are in a wooded area. The creek stones are white. One boy discovered a frog and is sharing the treasure with his friend, who responds enthusiastically.

COMMENTARY: This card shows the innocence and joy of childhood. There is nothing more exciting to these boys than their present moment and the discovery of a frog. They share this moment without expectation or any ego driven motive. They exist for the sheer pleasure of their time together. Children are amazingly generous. Their instincts are pure and they are not afraid to show their true feelings. The frog is strongly associated with the water element. It connects us with the world of emotions. The woods are the natural world that the children have no fear of expressing. White stones symbolize the purity and innocence of their intent.

IN A READING: Be in the moment. Recapture the innocence of childhood and let go of the stress of being an adult. Find someone to share this experience with, for no other reason than the joy of sharing. You could also be reconnected with childhood friends or memories or have feelings of nostalgia that need to be addressed. You could be dealing with something that has happened in your past or repeating a past behavior.

MEDITATION: I am not afraid to share my feelings.

DAILY READING: Play.

SEVEN OF WATER

Without doubt anything is possible.

PRIMARY CONCEPTS: Dreams, Imagination, Belief

DESCRIPTION: The Seven of Water depicts a young boy at the wheel of a yacht. The big blue captain's chair is behind him. He is too short to see over the wheel and the captain's hat he wears is way too big for him. The interior of the cabin is wood. The boat is tied to a pier with a yellow rope.

COMMENTARY: This card is about belief in our dreams. As children we often pretend we are grown up and in one profession or the other. We sometimes lose the ability to dream as we mature and settle for a life that may or may not be fulfilling. Children dream big because they have not yet learned there are limits to their dreams. If as adults we could capture that same imagination, we could retain our dreams and accomplish them as this child will do in the Nine of Water.

The blue chair symbolizes the seat of the imagination. It is surrounded by the wood interior representing the flexibility of the child's beliefs. The mind is what tethers our dreams like the yellow rope ties the boat to the dock.

IN A READING: There are no limits except the ones that you place on yourself. If you keep your dreams alive you can accomplish anything. It is time to take steps to make your dreams come true. Use your unlimited imagination. Daydreams can become delusions when we do not act upon them. This card could also represent the need to pay closer attention to dreams when you sleep. They may be offering you guidance.

MEDITATION: I believe anything is possible.

DAILY READING: Don't limit yourself. Believe you can and you will.

Eight of Water

Everything comes to an end.

Primary Concepts: Turning Point, Completion

Description: The Eight of Water shows an artist who has just completed his latest work, a painting of a fountain. He has turned from it and is putting away his tools into yellow containers. The brick arch frames his art. There is a stone floor beneath him. He wears blue.

Commentary: It is difficult to know when we are finished with something, when it is time to quit and move on. Even if the artist is not completely satisfied with his work, he knows he has done all he could and it is time to start something new. This process is sometimes difficult. Letting go, especially when there is emotional attachment involved, is hard. So many times we hold on to people, situations, or things long after we have exhausted our efforts or they no longer have a positive effect on us. We keep going back again and again to try to make changes or improve situations that are over. These efforts are unsuccessful and leave us feeling frustrated as if we have failed. It takes a great deal of emotional maturity to know when to quit. The fountain represents an emotional release. The arch threshold is a gateway to new creative endeavors. Yellow indicates the conscious decision he made to walk away and take with him only what he needs.

The stone floor beneath him supports his choice. Blue is the color of emotion.

IN A READING: You have done all you can and it is time to let go. This is an emotional turning point in your life. Move forward and don't look back. Be satisfied that your work is finished. This is the completion of a cycle in your life.

MEDITATION: I know when it is time to move on.

DAILY READING: Evaluate what you are holding on to. If there is nothing more you can do, you are done.

NINE OF WATER

Confidence fulfills dreams.

PRIMARY CONCEPTS: Confidence, Fulfillment

DESCRIPTION: The Nine of Water shows the child from the Seven of Water with his dream fulfilled. He is captain of his own boat and has grown into his hat. There is a big smile on his face. The sea is calm and the card is filled with the color blue.

COMMENTARY: This card demonstrates the power of believing in yourself and your dreams. The child from the Seven of Water had no doubt he would someday own his own boat. We all dream when we are children, but the difference is this child never let go of his. He turned it into a reality. The hat indicates how long he has held this dream. It wasn't fulfilled quickly but it was fulfilled. He had to grow into it. His smile expresses confidence, self-assuredness, and joy. The calm sea symbolizes the path before him, made smooth by his determination. The abundance of blue suggests he is master of his emotions.

IN A READING: Have confidence in yourself and your dreams will be fulfilled. Take the necessary steps to achieve your goals. Confidence is all you need. This card could also indicate overconfidence. Reconsider your situation.

MEDITATION: I have the confidence to fulfill my dreams.

DAILY READING: Today's a day to believe in yourself. An old dream can now be a new opportunity.

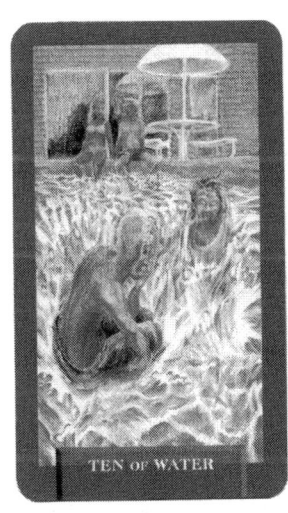

TEN OF WATER

True happiness is found in the joy of a loved one.

PRIMARY CONCEPTS: Happiness, Love, Family

DESCRIPTION: The Ten of Water depicts a family at play in their backyard swimming pool. The mom and dad sit on the side holding hands and watching their son and daughter splash each other in fun. The home has pink siding. There is a white patio set outside the sliding glass doors to the house.

COMMENTARY: There are times in life that are uncomplicated and happy. When one of these moments occurs we should keep our attention there and cherish it. There is no hidden agenda here, just fun and love and family. These times renew us, revitalize us and build strong relationships with those who support us. The family is all touching the water demonstrating their emotional connection with one another. Their home is built with love indicated by the color pink. The white umbrella symbolizes the purity that envelops this moment. The doors are transparent, like they are with one another.

IN A READING: A happy time is at hand or coming soon. You should be ready to enjoy it to the fullest. Savor the moment. This card could represent a family gathering or successful family relationships. Spend time with those you love.

MEDITATION: I give and receive love freely.

DAILY READING: Spend time with people you love today. This connection sustains you.

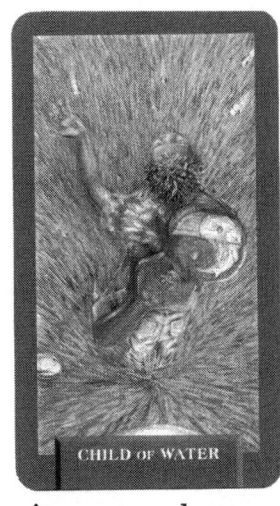

Child of Water

Awakening creativity must be nurtured.

Primary Concepts: Sensitivity, Awakening Emotions

Description: The Child of Water shows a young boy standing in tall grass reaching up with his hand to catch a raindrop. There is a purple guitar case slung over his back displaying the yin/yang symbol, a dolphin and a rose. He wears blue.

Commentary: This card shows the beginnings of creativity and sensitivity. All of the Child cards in Today's Journey Tarot are meant to express the essence of the element of each suit in its infancy. Water is the element of the emotions. He reaches out to the raindrop to capture his budding emotional nature. This child has an awakening desire to make music. The yin/yang symbol is the balance this expression will bring into his life. Dolphins are sensitive and gentle creatures and a rose symbolizes the subconscious mind. The purple case is the promise of mastery. Without the sensitive souls willing to share their imaginations with the world it would be a bleak and stark place to live.

In a Reading: This card could represent either a person (male or female) or a situation. The person is sensitive, gentle, emotionally naïve, curious, and spiritual. Be aware of those individuals and do everything you can to support their talent. The card can also represent a situation that requires sensitivity. Someone may be acting immaturely or you may need to look at a situation more creatively. Creative expression is a spiritual gift that should be encouraged and nurtured. It allows you to honestly share your emotional self and for some this is the only way they can. It also assures that sensitivity and the creative spirit lies dormant within everyone, just waiting to be awakened.

MEDITATION: I allow my creativity to flow.

DAILY READING: Expose yourself to the arts. Stimulate your creative spirit.

YOUTH OF WATER

Love life.

PRIMARY CONCEPTS: Outpouring of Love, Emotional Intensity

DESCRIPTION: The Youth of Water shows a young man on a white surfboard riding the waves. He is surrounded by the blue ocean. His right hand reaches into the wave while his left hand skims the surface. He is wearing a puka shell necklace and a blue surfboard leash around his right ankle.

COMMENTARY: This card expresses love of life. The surfer is enjoying this moment to the fullest, soaking up all of the excitement. He is not ready to commit to anything or anyone. He may appear to be somewhat irresponsible but his intent is pure. The white surfboard that supports him represents his innocence. The waters of emotion completely surround him. They are the force that drives his momentum, but his only contact with them is his right, giving hand. His left hand skims the surface of the water indicating that he freely expresses his emotions but is reluctant to receive them from others. Puka shells represent good luck which is what he relies on. He leashes himself to the surfboard to push the limits of his experience.

IN A READING: This card could represent either a person (male or female) or a situation. If this card represents a person, he or she is a big, loveable kid. Do not expect a long lasting relationship or a dependable friend. Do enjoy the outpouring of love and exhilaration that comes into your life. The card can also represent an intensely emotional situation that may be exciting and fun but short lived. It could be a new love that is transient. Proceed with caution or just enjoy the ride.

MEDITATION: I celebrate life to the fullest.

DAILY READING: Today is a good day to have fun. It could be your lucky day.

Mother of Water

Repressed emotions will surface eventually.

Primary Concepts: Reflective, Subconscious, Hidden Emotions

Description: The Mother of Water shows a woman staring out of a cabin window at the rain. It runs down the window panes. She holds a white cup of steaming liquid as she gazes out into the world. Her sweater is blue.

Commentary: The Mother of Water prefers to be alone with her own emotions hidden deep within. She does not share them easily. Although she is gentle and caring with others she does not let them know who she really is. Perhaps she is afraid of their judgment or simply doesn't feel it is right to burden someone else with her problems. She chooses to live in a cabin, preferring isolation. The water streaked window further emphasizes the emotional veil through which she sees the world. Her emotions, represented by the oversized cup, are impossible to ignore. Yet the cup covers her heart, to keep her deepest feelings hidden. Her comfortable, light blue sweater reflects her gentle soul.

In a Reading: This card could represent either a person (male or female) or a situation. The person is difficult to really get to know because she keeps a lot of herself hidden. She is more at home in her subconscious than in the ordinary world. She prefers to be alone or with a small group of trusted people. This card can also represent a situation where it may be time to let someone else share the burden. Too much is being kept bottled up inside and it needs to be released. It can also indicate a time for reflection is needed. In either case emotions need to be released to find balance.

MEDITATION: I do not fear expressing my emotions.

DAILY READING: Share your emotions with someone you trust. It is time to ease your burden.

FATHER OF WATER

Love is healing.

PRIMARY CONCEPTS: Nurturing, Emotionally Connected, Healing

DESCRIPTION: The Father of Water shows a man sitting on a wooden dock that stretches out over the ocean. He sits above the water but his feet are submerged. There is a silver food bucket beside him labeled "Dolphin Rescue." The same logo appears on the left sleeve of his wetsuit in purple. The sleeves of the suit are white. A dolphin rises up out of the water to meet his extended hand. The ocean all around him reflects the pink sky.

COMMENTARY: The Father of Water is not afraid to be a nurturer and express his emotions by caring for one of the world's most gentle creatures. The card is alive with blues and pinks suggesting the healing love the man and the dolphin share. His feet in the water symbolize his understanding of emotions and his ability to share them with others. His right or giving hand reaches out to touch the dolphin. The white sleeve indicates the purity of his intent. From the silver bucket he provides the emotional and physical support the dolphin needs. The purple logo symbolizes the mastery of his emotions. The wooden dock that supports him stretches out over the water. His emotional maturity allows him to feel comfortable surrounded by the sea.

IN A READING: This card could represent either a person (male or female) or a situation. The person is emotionally mature and available. He is creative and gentle, perhaps a healer who is not afraid to share his emotions. The card could also represent a situation where nurturing is needed. Too many times the cries of those in need go unheeded in our world because we are just too afraid to get involved. This card says to let go of that fear and extend a hand. Get in touch with your emotions. The reward comes when a beautiful being nudges your hand in thanks and you realize you shared the most powerful healing energy of all, love.

MEDITATION: I am loving and nurturing to all.

DAILY READING: Help someone today. Even if it is just with a smile.

Air

One of Air

The mind, like a coastal house, can either be open to the sea breeze or closed in fear.

Primary Concepts: Clarity, Truth, Intellect

Description: The One of Air shows yellow sea oats blowing in the wind on a coastline. The sky is blue and clear and the sand is white.

Commentary: This card expresses the power and randomness of our minds. Air gives life and is the element of thought. Its color yellow represents the intellect and wind is its strongest expression. Uncontrolled thoughts can race through our minds like the wind through sea oats, causing both positive and negative results. Negative random thoughts can produce depression or fear. Positive thoughts give birth to new ideas, answers to problems and an optimistic attitude.

In a Reading: Be aware of your thoughts and direct them in productive ways. This card represents a new idea, truth, thought or clarification of an existing thought or idea.

Meditation: I control my thoughts, they do not control me.

Daily Reading: Be aware of negative thoughts today. When they occur, replace them with positive ones.

Two of Air

It is difficult to make a decision without seeing the options.

Primary Concepts: Decision, Responsibility, Informed Choice

Description: The Two of Air shows a young girl playing a carnival dart game. There are only two yellow balloons left for her to hit. The girl has her hand over her eyes so she cannot see where she is throwing. A carnival worker gives her a thumbs up. She wears a grey hoodie and stands on a sawdust road.

Commentary: Sometimes we drive ourselves crazy trying to figure out the right thing to do. We often feel like this whenever we have decisions or choices to make. If we only knew the outcome our choice would be a lot easier, but we never do. We even try to get someone else to make decisions for us whenever we can. We make decisions all day long with each action we take. Some turn out fine and sometimes we regret we hadn't chosen better. We are meant to make our own decisions so we can learn what we need to and then move on. The girl believes she is giving up responsibility for her actions. However, she has already made a choice. The two yellow balloons symbolize the alternatives open to her. The carnival worker offers her encouragement she cannot see. Grey is the color of doubt. A sawdust road is only temporary.

IN A READING: Open your eyes and gather as much information as possible about your choice, then make an informed decision without speculating on the outcome. Take responsibility for your actions.

MEDITATION: I recognize that there are no wrong choices.

DAILY READING: Make a choice you have been putting off. Let go of fear and doubt and just decide.

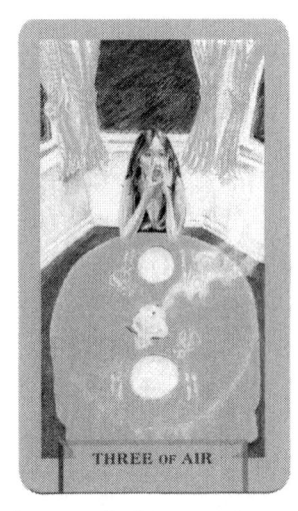

THREE OF AIR

Expectations can often lead to disappointment.

PRIMARY CONCEPTS: Separation, Disappointment

DESCRIPTION: The Three of Air depicts a young woman sitting alone at a dining table set for two. The candle in the middle of the table has burned down to smoke. She is staring off with a look of disbelief on her face. The predominant color in the card is yellow. The window behind her shows the darkness outside.

COMMENTARY: Disappointment is something we must learn to live with in our lives. The woman has a choice to make. She can be devastated by her experience and suffer emotional scars that could effect her for a long time or she can decide to release her feelings of unhappiness and go on with her life. Disappointment is separation from desire.

The sooner we learn to accept what happens instead of pining for something that cannot be, the happier we will become and the more productive. Yellow, the color of thought suggests that the way she is thinking has created her sorrow. The extinguished candle indicates her loss of hope. She is bringing the darkness in.

IN A READING: Something didn't turn out like you expected. Let it go. If it didn't happen like you anticipated, it wasn't supposed to. This could be a separation from something or someone you desire. Perhaps your expectations are misdirected. How long you suffer disappointment is your choice. This experience could be the best thing for you.

MEDITATION: I release expectations and choose satisfaction.

DAILY READING: Things may not go as planned today. Rethink your situation and choose happiness.

FOUR OF AIR

There are times when rest is the only action required.

PRIMARY CONCEPTS: Healing, Rest, Respite

DESCRIPTION: The Four of Air shows a boxer between rounds. He is taking a mandatory rest before going back into the fight. He is a little beat up but his trainer is caring for him. Soon he will be ready to return to the match. He is wearing yellow trunks.

COMMENTARY: Most of us rarely get enough rest or down time. In sports, time outs are required and expected but in life we often have little time to relax. It is important to recharge and refill ourselves physically, mentally, emotionally, and spiritually. The trainer represents the loving care and encouragement we can give ourselves during times of respite, even if it is only for a few minutes. During these times we heal from the stress of our lives. The boxer's yellow trunks suggest that his activity is more mental than physical. He is preparing to go back to the fight.

IN A READING: Stop, take a break and nurture yourself before going back into the daily routine. Allow healing to occur. Gather your strength for what is to come. Accept the assistance being offered.

MEDITATION: There is nothing I need to do right now.

DAILY READING: Take time out today to just rest.

FIVE OF AIR

Victory gained through deceit is fleeting.

PRIMARY CONCEPTS: Temporary Victory, Deceit

DESCRIPTION: The Five of Air shows a used car salesman. He is holding the paperwork of his latest deal. The family drives away in their new car. The signs around the lot read, "Bad Credit, No Credit, No Problem". There are red, yellow and orange pennants circling the lot. A small area of green grass is restricted by a chained barrier. The contract he holds and the price sticker on the car's window are both yellow.

COMMENTARY: The signs suggest great deals will be made at this lot no matter what your financial situation. The salesman has a satisfied look on his face. His truth shifts like the pennants that blow freely in the breeze. Under these conditions he will not be successful. His gain is only temporary. Unfortunately we must deal with unscrupulous people. They seem to be ever present in our lives. The tales they tell and the justifications they make are not honest. Ultimately the responsibility for our well being is ours. Caution must be taken to ensure we are not being deceived. If so we can choose to walk away, no matter how good the deal. The contract and the price sticker are yellow, representing the intellect, which the salesman has manipulated for his own gain. The green grass is the only symbol of growth in the card, and it is restricted.

In a Reading: Be careful. You are vulnerable to dishonesty. Examine your decisions carefully. Read the fine print. Be aware of who you are dealing with. It is also important to determine if you are the deceiver, being dishonest with yourself or somebody else. A deceitful victory is temporary. Deception and dishonesty are a terrible waste of thought.

MEDITATION: I am honest with myself and others.

DAILY READING: Caution is advised today. Someone may not be honest with you.

SIX OF AIR

Sometimes a leap of faith is necessary.

PRIMARY CONCEPTS: Journey, Leap of Faith, New Beginning

DESCRIPTION: The Six of Air shows a family packed in their vehicle and heading down the road. The yellow car is moving in the same direction as a flock of geese in the distance. The divided highway is bordered on all sides by grass and young trees. Clouds can be seen in the reflection of the back window but the sky ahead is clear. A child holds a paper airplane out the passenger window and the license plate reads, "R3N3W".

COMMENTARY: *Today's Journey* is the life we lead every day. Over and over again we pack up and move on. Sometimes the move is a monumental and life changing leap of faith and sometimes it is as simple as throwing out an old pair of shoes. Whatever is not working can be left behind and we can start over. It is not as easy as it sounds, but the opportunity always exists even if we cannot see it or are afraid of it. The geese leading the way suggest it is always better to follow our instincts. We know when it is time to make a move and it is a waste of energy to postpone or worry about it. The grass and trees express the new growth that comes with change. The clear sky ahead assures they are moving in the right direction. The paper airplane the child holds symbolizes the playfulness of freedom. Renewal is indicated by the license plate. The car is positive thought manifested.

IN A READING: Take a leap of faith to a new beginning. This is a new step or the next step in a positive direction. Take only what you need and let the rest go. Travel may be indicated, possibly a move.

MEDITATION: I trust my journey is moving me in the right direction.

DAILY READING: You know what you need to do. Today's the day to do it. Begin your new journey.

Seven of Air

Nothing can be stolen without consent.

Primary Concepts: Theft, Cheating, Dishonesty

Description: The Seven of Air shows two boys in school taking a test. They are sitting at the same table in the cafeteria. One boy is cheating by looking at the other one's paper. They are both dressed in school uniforms. The cheater's tie is loosened and the top of his shirt is unbuttoned. His feet are not firmly planted on the floor. The school mascot, a yellow eagle, is prominent behind them on the wall.

Commentary: We are all subject to being victimized. The thief is stealing knowledge that doesn't belong to him. If we create our own reality, nothing can be stolen from us without our consent, whether we are conscious of it or not. Be aware that thieves lurk in all kinds of places and seize the opportunity to take advantage of our vulnerability. The cheater's attire demonstrates his relaxed attitude towards rules. Unlike the other student his feet are not grounded. The yellow eagle, poised to snatch its prey, suggests that dishonest behavior looms large in our society and is always ready for its next victim. Material theft is only one aspect of this card. More often it concerns theft of time or emotions.

In a Reading: This card is about thievery and dishonesty. Someone may be trying to steal something from you, monopolize your time or use guilt to control your emotions. It is time to be extra cautious. This card may suggest that you are the thief. Take a hard look at your own behavior.

Meditation: I do not allow deception in my life.

Daily Reading: Be careful today. Do not let yourself be taken advantage of.

Eight of Air

Fear is a self-imposed prison.

Primary Concepts: Despair, Fear, Imprisonment

Description: The Eight of Air shows a woman huddled on a brown couch in her home. There are multiple locks securing the front door. Her head is buried in her knees. She wears a gray sweat suit. Outside her window a yellow hot air balloon is rising up into the sky. The grass in front of her home is yellow.

Commentary: This card symbolizes the imprisonment of fear, which immobilizes, confuses, and confines. Fear is a natural impulse. Our fight or flight instincts save lives. This useful tool can become a plaything of the mind which then distorts an advantage into a burden. The woman's focus is on her gray sweat suit. She can see nothing but her own despair. Brown is a foundation color. Hers is locked in this room. Locks are usually protection, but her extreme use of them symbolizes overprotective thought. Across the street the green grass represents normal growth, hers has withered. The balloon indicates the uplifting thoughts which could offer her freedom.

IN A READING: Do not let fear imprison you. Do not become overwhelmed by despair. If you cannot see a way out of a situation, recognize it is self imposed. You must look within yourself for the way out. Change your thoughts and free yourself. Lift yourself up.

MEDITATION: I do not allow fear to control me.

DAILY READING: Recognize the limits you are experiencing are your own creation. Take a step today to free yourself.

NINE OF AIR

Worry is a trap set by the mind.

PRIMARY CONCEPTS: Worry, Sleeplessness, Trapped

DESCRIPTION: The Nine of Air shows a woman at her kitchen table, obviously distraught over the pile of bills stretched out in front of her. A checkbook lays closed on the table. Her large coffee cup is empty and her ashtray is full. The kitchen is dark and she is wearing a yellow housecoat. The refrigerator and counter top are chartreuse. There is a caged gray cockatiel next to her.

COMMENTARY: Worry is a useless emotion that serves no purpose. It eats up our energy and fills our mind with ineffectual thoughts that do not offer solutions. We worry about everything, whether it is an actual situation in our lives or the thousands of what ifs that plagues us every day. We become trapped by these thoughts just as the bird is imprisoned by its cage. The coffee cup and ashtray show she's been here a long time trying to figure out what to do. She can't see a solution to her troubles. The bills spread before her signify the problems keeping her awake. Chartreuse represents the mind's interference with growth.

IN A READING: This card represents worry or sleeplessness. If you put worry aside you will be able to come up with answers to your problems. Deal with these issues rather than letting them overwhelm you. Every problem has a solution. Help may be needed for a sleep disorder.

MEDITATION: I will put worry aside and find solutions.

DAILY READING: You may feel overwhelmed today. Deal with things one at a time instead of all at once.

Ten of Air

For every ending there is always a new beginning.

Primary Concepts: Renewal, Perspective, End of Cycle

Description: The Ten of Air shows a devastated neighborhood. We don't know what caused the destruction but buildings are gone or damaged and the land is bare. Yellow butterflies have gathered on the stone foundation of a former building.

Commentary: This card expresses the hope of renewal. No matter what happens to us, at the end of every cycle there is always another beginning. Although the land and buildings have been damaged and deserted, the butterflies have chosen this spot to rest. Butterflies signify transformation. We can view the scene as one of destruction, or change our perspective to that of the butterfly by looking forward to a rebirth. It is not about what happens to us, it is about our perspective.

In a Reading: Focus on the positive. The worst is over and it is time to look forward to a new beginning. You may not be able to see past the current situation, but the opportunity for renewal is assured.

Meditation: I choose to be positive.

Daily Reading: Get a new perspective today on the situation you are facing. Optimism creates opportunities.

Child of Air

New ideas change the world.

Primary Concepts: New Ideas, Optimism

Description: The Child of Air shows a little girl flying a yellow kite. She has just gotten it up into the air. The nose is diving and the string is not taut. She is standing in a grassy area of a park.

Commentary: This card expresses the excitement and wonder of an awakened mind. It is like learning how to fly. The Child of Air's thoughts are still immature and like the yellow kite could change direction at any moment, depending on how the wind blows. There are no restrictions to her mind. She is still too young to be hampered by the limitations of doubt and fear that bind more matured minds. The kite represents thought. Its string is the grounding necessary to turn ideas into productive realities. Without the string the kite would not fly. The yellow/green grass signifies the growth that unrestricted thought can accomplish.

In a Reading: This card could represent a person (male or female) or a situation. The person is optimistic. She could be indecisive, but full of ideas. She needs guidance to follow through. In a situation, let your mind be free to explore new thoughts and ideas. It is possible an idea will take flight and offer an exciting new direction for your life or even change the world.

MEDITATION: I do not limit my thoughts.

DAILY READING: A new thought or idea today could have positive results. Spend some time brainstorming.

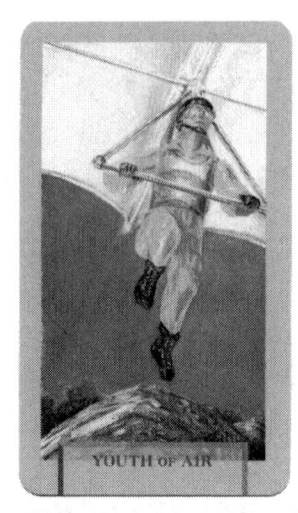

YOUTH OF AIR

An adventurous mind overcomes adversity.

PRIMARY CONCEPTS: Daring, Reckless, Independent

DESCRIPTION: The Youth of Air shows a young woman just lifting off of a rock cliff in a hang glider. She is wearing a yellow jump suit. The glider is white. The sky behind her is blue.

COMMENTARY: This card expresses the adventurous spirit of youth. When we are young we tend to be reckless, fearless, and independent. We are ready to try anything at a moment's notice and rarely worry about the consequences. As we mature and become aware of danger and responsibility, these exploits become less frequent. The Youth of Air is well prepared for her adventure. She has thought it through, acquired the proper gear and learned the correct form. The only thing she doesn't have is experience, which could be dangerous. Her yellow suit indicates the boldness of thought which guides her. She utilizes air (her intellect) to sustain and support her. The white glider represents innocence. Her lack of experience does not deter her. The sky is her limit.

IN A READING: This card could represent a person (male or female) or a situation. The person is independent, intellectual, daring, and adventurous. It is her lack of experience that makes her reckless. In a situation you should loosen up and take some risks. That doesn't mean to act irresponsibly. Do what you need to do to be prepared, but there are no completely safe risks. Air is the element of thought. Think it through, be as prepared as possible, and then jump.

MEDITATION: I am not afraid to take risks.

DAILY READING: Do not let lack of experience deter you from trying something new.

MOTHER OF AIR

Truth is the final judgment.

PRIMARY CONCEPTS: Truth, Intellect, Judgment

DESCRIPTION: The Mother of Air shows a judge sitting at her courtroom bench. She looks at us the same way as the golden raptor at the large window looks into the scene. She wears a yellow collar, black robe, and has her arms crossed in front of her. The wood surrounding her has a purple cast. She sits in a high back black leather chair. There is an American flag behind her.

COMMENTARY: This card represents hard facts not swayed by emotion. There are times when we need to understand the truth of a situation so we can deal with it and then move on. The Mother of Air always sees the truth and cannot be fooled or persuaded from it. She can be perceived as cold and hard but that is her job. Sometimes when the truth is staring us right in the face we are too emotionally involved to see it. A judge must weigh only the facts and then make a decision. The raptor symbolizes the ability to see every detail. Like her, nothing escapes its gaze. The window suggests she sees the world in the same way she does the courtroom. The yellow collar represents her sharp intellect and the black robe and crossed arms protect her from unwanted emotion. Purple, the color of mastery surrounds her. The chair supports her control. The flag is a source of pride and inspiration, strength and unity.

IN A READING: This card could represent a person (male or female) or a situation. The person is not swayed by emotions but uses intellect to discern the truth. She could be perceived as harsh or stern especially if lied to. Experience has taught her to be strong and smart. In a situation you need to separate the false from the truth. Look at the circumstances clearly and logically. The answer lies in the details. Do not let your emotions affect your logic. Use what you learn to make your own judgments.

MEDITATION: I open myself to truth.

DAILY READING: The truth is there for you to see. Look for it today.

Father of Air

Analytical thinking produces proper action.

Primary Concepts: Analytical, Detachment, Integrity

Description: The Father of Air depicts a pilot in control of his plane. The controls are highlighted in yellow. His seat is gray. He wears a blue uniform with three yellow chevrons on the shoulder.

Commentary: Pilots must remain calm in any situation. The Father of Air is detached and analytical, which is why he is so comfortable in the sky. He is very at ease with the complex control panel and knows just what to do. He achieved the position he is in because his integrity is beyond reproach. Logic is the way to reach him. The controls represent his attention to detail. Gray, the color of doubt is behind him. The light blue uniform suggests he is content in his role. Chevrons denote rank and length of service.

In a Reading: This card could represent a person (male or female) or a situation. The person is goal oriented and intelligent. He could come across as cool and emotionally unavailable because emotion is not something he is comfortable with. Appeal to his logic. He is a detail oriented, honest worker who responds instinctively. He could be controlling because he believes he is right. In a situation cool detachment is necessary. Step back and look at the circumstances from a different perspective. It is possible emotions are clouding your judgment. You need to be honest with yourself or someone else. Take control.

MEDITATION: I see the world with detachment and honesty.

DAILY READING: You know what you need to do. Take control of the situation today.

EARTH

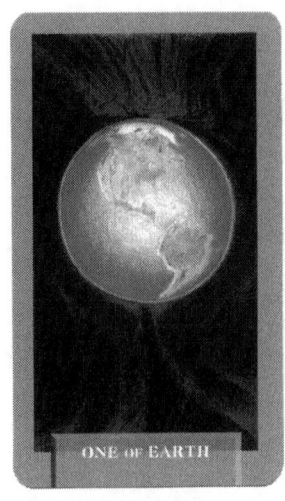

One of Earth

Abundance, like the Earth's bounty, never ceases.

Primary Concepts: Abundance, Growth, Grounding

Description: The One of Earth depicts the Western Hemisphere of our beautiful planet in all of its glory. It is seen from space surrounded by its magnetosphere.

Commentary: The Ones in Today's Journey Tarot all express each Element in its ultimate influence. Our planet supports us as we grow and we are part of its splendor. This card reminds us there are no limits. We can achieve anything we desire because the Earth provides for us. As we nurture the Earth, we also nurture ourselves to unlimited possibilities.

In a Reading: This card indicates a new cycle of growth and prosperity. It represents abundance, stability, growth, and power. It may suggest a need for grounding which is a practical focus on the task at hand.

Meditation: I am abundant.

Daily Reading: Ground yourself. Spend some time in nature today.

Two of Earth

Simplification improves balance.

Primary Concepts: Juggling, Balance

Description: The Two of Earth shows a woman very busy at her job. She is waiting on customers behind the diner's counter. She is also in the middle of making change, overseeing orders, pouring coffee and supervising her daughter doing homework. She wears a brown apron, her daughter wears green and white. Behind her the décor is light purple and green. The floor is white tile. Yellow tickets hang on the rail. Breakfast orders are ready to be served.

Commentary: This card is an accurate depiction of modern life. We multi-task all day long taking care of work, home, family, and other responsibilities. Our attention is divided and we have difficulty getting anything done. We try to juggle everything all at once. Sometimes this is impossible and leads to frustration and exhaustion. Balancing everything is not easy, but the woman is determined to accomplish it all. Her brown apron represents the grounding she needs, while her daughter's clothes reflect growth and innocence. The décor's colors symbolize a lack of balance, practicality, and order. She stands on white tile, a foundation suggesting her intention is pure. The yellow tickets indicate her mind is full early in the morning.

In a Reading: Balance is needed. You are juggling too much. Prioritize and manage your life in a way that is not so harried and overwhelming. To accomplish anything take care of one thing at a time. It is your choice to be the juggler. How long can you keep it up?

MEDITATION: I choose to simplify my life.

DAILY READING: Evaluate your day. Do each task according to its importance and release what is unnecessary.

THREE OF EARTH

Talent should be recognized.

PRIMARY CONCEPTS: Recognition, Artistry

DESCRIPTION: The Three of Earth depicts the illustrator of Today's Journey Tarot, Christopher Wilkey. He stands with a lighted exhibit of his art, including cards from the deck and a large cast bronze sculpture of a merkaba on a white base. Chris is wearing earth tones.

COMMENTARY: This card expresses the appreciation and recognition all artists deserve for entertaining and enlightening. The amount of effort and dedication Chris displayed in creating more that seventy eight images of Today's Journey Tarot over several years was phenomenal. This card recognizes we are all creative and use our talents in work, relationships, play and every aspect of life. Everyone deserves to be recognized for the contribution they make but it is not always necessary to look to others for that acknowledgement. It is important to see it in ourselves and encourage it in others. Creativity must be nurtured to grow. The clothes he wears represents his abundance of talent and he is grounded in his belief in himself.

IN A READING: If you are getting the recognition you deserve be proud of it. If not, seek it. You need to recognize your own ability. Tap into creativity and see what you can accomplish. It could also represent someone around you may need to be encouraged or recognized in the arts.

MEDITATION: I recognize my own talent.

DAILY READING: Put your abilities on display. Show others what you can do.

FOUR OF EARTH

There is more to the world than just the physical.

PRIMARY CONCEPTS: Self-Absorption, Self-Satisfaction

DESCRIPTION: The Four of Earth shows a very well dressed woman admiring her image in a gold framed mirror. The dressing room is filled with clothes and shoes. She is wearing diamonds and a full length fur coat over her green dress. The floor is purple.

COMMENTARY: We often forget we are not merely the image we see in the mirror. We spend countless hours perfecting this persona and displaying it to the world. There is much more to us than what is reflected by our perceived image of ourselves. Because we are part of the material world, we can easily become deceived by outward appearances. Striving for perfection and material goods can consume our lives. It is what is inside of us, our spiritual nature that truly sustains us. Wealth, good looks, or power are only temporary. The woman in the mirror has material richness. She is satisfied with herself and her wealth but the stone she prizes covers her heart, symbolizing she is closed off to everything else. She refuses to let go of her attachment to opulence. She wears a green dress which represents growth and abundance. However the dead weight of the fur coat entraps her.

IN A READING: No matter what your station in life, you need to reexamine your values and seek freedom from earthly entrapments. You may be holding on too tightly to material things. Release attachments. This card could also indicate being too stingy with emotions, time, or energy. All you see is your reflection of yourself.

MEDITATION: I reach beneath the surface to find my true self.

DAILY READING: Make certain you are seeing beyond your own needs today.

Five of Earth

Something new is always being offered.

Primary Concepts: Loss, Grief, Stagnation

Description: The Five of Earth shows a woman sitting in front of a stone monument. She is obviously grieving. A white feather floats down from the sky behind her. She sits on a stone bench, wearing all black. The sky is gray and the grass and bushes are only partially green.

Commentary: We are often blinded by grief. Our lives are subject to loss. We lose people, jobs, relationships, animal friends, homes, favorite possessions, and on and on. A period of grief is healing and necessary but often we have difficulty letting go because we remain focused on what we have lost. The imposing stone monument is cold, hard, and unchanging. She has her back to the feather which represents the promise of hope, lightness, and freedom. We will never regain what we've lost but there is a new beginning if we reach out for it. Black is a symbol of her grief. The gray sky is limitation and the partially green grass, stagnated growth.

In a Reading: You have suffered a loss or are experiencing a period of stagnation. It is time to move on. From your perspective of grief you cannot see what else is being offered. Hope and freedom are available.

MEDITATION: I look for new beginnings.

DAILY READING: See beyond the present situation. Begin making plans for the future.

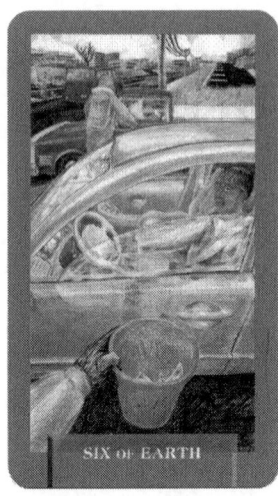

SIX OF EARTH

Give without expectation.

PRIMARY CONCEPTS: Charity

DESCRIPTION: The Six of Earth shows a driver in a gray car stopped at a busy intersection. A volunteer is holding a green collection bucket that says "Give" to the car window for a donation. The driver reluctantly complies. The volunteers, dressed in yellow, are in other lanes and intersections as well.

COMMENTARY: People ask us for things all the time. Although we give, we often do so without a charitable heart. The volunteers are soliciting the drivers for money who feel they have no choice. This card says there is nothing wrong with asking for help but oftentimes we ask in such a way that causes resentment. It is good to give of ourselves, our time, and our money. But do it freely and without expectation or resentment. The green bucket represents balanced giving but the gray car suggests the driver's hesitation to give.

In a Reading: Give, not because it is expected of you but because you have enough to share. Contribute because you want to without obligation or expecting anything in return. When it is your time to ask for help, it will be freely given.

MEDITATION: I give of myself freely and without expectation.

DAILY READING: You will always have enough to share. What can you share today?

SEVEN OF EARTH

Don't spend today living for tomorrow.

PRIMARY CONCEPTS: Patience

DESCRIPTION: The Seven of Earth shows a girl sitting at the mail box with her back against the post. She stares longingly down the road waiting for the mail. The weather is chilly and she wraps her arms around her knees for warmth. The sky is gray.

COMMENTARY: There are times when we have to be patient. We do everything necessary to ensure an outcome, and wait for that to occur. However we don't want to spend our whole lives waiting for something. We wait to grow up, get out of school, get married, and get a good job. We are always living our lives for the future. The problem is the future rarely fulfills our expectations. We use all that time waiting when we could be living the life we have right now. When the future comes we just start waiting for something else. Without putting in the effort and work to create the outcome we become frustrated that our goals are not fulfilled. The girl knows the letter will come because she has done everything necessary to ensure its delivery. The gray winter season is a time of dormancy while we wait for the blue skies of spring. Her green scarf represents the growth the message will provide when the time is right. She also wears orange, the color of sociability suggesting she could spend this time with others instead of alone at the mailbox.

IN A READING: Don't have an expectation without taking the steps to create it. If everything has been done to ensure a successful outcome, be patient. Focus on living your life in the present.

MEDITATION: I live my life for today.

DAILY READING: What you are waiting for may not come today. It's not time yet. Enjoy today for what it is.

Eight of Earth

Effort yields prosperity.

Primary Concepts: Skill, Effort, Prosperity

Description: The Eight of Earth shows a jeweler at work creating his designs. The tools of his trade are laid on the table before him as well as the stones he has chosen to use in his jewelry. These stones are the colors of the chakras: red, orange, yellow, green, blue, indigo, and violet. He wears an optivisor. The shelving behind him is green.

Commentary: This card shows the ingenuity and creativity of craftsmen who build beautiful works of art as well as objects we utilize every day. The jeweler learned his trade from a master so his skill will provide him with the prosperity he desires. He knows instinctively he must also connect with the creativity of spirit so he chooses the chakra colors to open that link. All of us have skills and talents that can be cultivated. It takes effort, study, training, and a lot of practice but eventually we can master a trade. The tools represent his accumulation of knowledge. The optivisor symbolizes the focus needed to create success. He doesn't loose sight of his goals. Green is the color of prosperity, balance, and growth.

In a Reading: Use your skills to bring prosperity and abundance into your life. This card could also represent a new vocation that requires going to school or training. You could turn your talent into a business with the right tools. Focus, apply yourself, and succeed.

MEDITATION: My efforts create prosperity.

DAILY READING: Hard work pays off today.

NINE OF EARTH

Abundance and independence are obtained through self-assuredness.

PRIMARY CONCEPTS: Abundance, Independence, Security

DESCRIPTION: The Nine of Earth depicts an equestrian and her horse. The woman is well dressed in riding gear and her left hand rests on the horse's neck. She holds the reins in her right hand. They are in a field of tall green grass. The sky is gray.

COMMENTARY: This card expresses independence and abundance. It also suggests self-reliance and self-assuredness. The rider is at ease with her horse and controls him with gentleness rather than force. She has no doubt in her ability and needs nothing else to control him. The animal bows his head to her mastery. Her affection for the horse is obvious by her touch. She is grounded, with both feet firmly on the earth. The colors she wears and the horse's coat are harmonious with the earth's energy, which sustains her. The tall, green grass emphasizes the abundant nature of this scene. She has her back to the gray sky.

IN A READING: You have everything under control and will achieve the abundance and security you desire. Have no doubt in your ability. Independence is the result of self-assuredness.

MEDITATION: I am the master of my destiny.

DAILY READING: The decision you make today is the correct one. Do not doubt it.

TEN OF EARTH

The past is a story that needs to be told.

PRIMARY CONCEPTS: Legacy, Bounty, Cycles of Life

DESCRIPTION: The Ten of Earth shows a grandfather telling stories to his grandchildren who are engrossed in his tales. A family dinner is being prepared and other adults are busy in the background setting the table, bringing out food, or just relaxing. Both of the children are wearing green. There is a yellow merkaba shaped chandelier over the dining room table. The floor and furniture reflect purple.

COMMENTARY: There is so much to learn from the legacy of those who have gone before, but we are impatient with the past. It seems irrelevant to our world today. A lot has changed but what our ancestors have to teach has nothing to do with technology, the latest fashion, or entertainment trends. Their experience in living and the basic valuable lessons they have learned do not change. The world continues to evolve but human beings deal with the same issues lifetime after lifetime. History repeats over and over. Only the names change. The grandfather tells stories of long ago. The meal being prepared is not the true bounty here. Other adults pay no attention and are distracted by the day's activities. Green clothing reflects the growth occurring within the children. The chandelier suggests what they learn transcends this moment and transforms them. Purple symbolizes mastery, imagination, and spirituality.

IN A READING: A legacy is being passed to you. The cycle of life continues. It is your choice how you use this bounty. Look to elders for advice and listen to their wisdom. There is value in their experience. The answers you seek could be offered from your own past. They could have occurred in another lifetime.

MEDITATION: I learn from the past.

DAILY READING: Seek the wisdom of someone with more experience than you. Learn from it.

Child of Earth

Knowledge enlightens the mind.

Primary Concepts: Student, Growth, Learning

Description: The Child of Earth shows a little girl at a school Science Fair. She is reading a book. There are exhibits on tables up and down the aisle. People are milling about. The shiny tile floor reflects the lights. She is wearing a green sweater and shoes.

Commentary: This card is about the pursuit of knowledge. The girl is a student who is always open to learning something new. She is very curious about everything and loves to research new subjects. When we open ourselves to more of what the world has to offer we experience the growth and rewards of learning. Only by stretching our ideas and enhancing our talent can we grow towards our potential. At the Science Fair the girl is learning about her environment. The fair represents the accumulated knowledge available. She learns from experience and must see to believe. The book represents her focus on the search for information. She doesn't give up until she finds the answers she seeks. Knowledge enlightens the mind like the lights illuminate the room.

In a Reading: This card could represent a person (male or female) or a situation. The person is studious, curious, persistent, and open-minded. She may be going to school or need to go. She enjoys learning and the steady progress of education. In a situation it is time for you to learn something new. This is a period of learning in whatever form that may be. Go back to school, take classes in a subject that interests you or just read and teach yourself a new skill. You must learn in order to grow.

MEDITATION: I expand my mind through the pursuit of knowledge.

DAILY READING: Learn something new today. It is up to you to find the answer.

YOUTH OF EARTH

Stability is required to be productive.

PRIMARY CONCEPTS: Stability, Productivity

DESCRIPTION: The Youth of Earth shows a young man working as a cave guide. He is explaining formations to the visitors. His right hand is on a stalactite and his left gestures to the crowd. He wears yellow and green.

COMMENTARY: This card expresses the enterprise of youth. The Youth of Earth is a stable and productive young man who has chosen a job reflecting the endurance of these qualities. The cave is carved from the earth itself. It is strong and constant and slow to change. He believes in the principles of hard work and will exhibit these qualities the rest of his life. He is focused and driven to succeed at a young age. This desire could overshadow other aspects of his life. He could become a very critical and difficult boss or neglect relationships as he drives himself to be the best. He gives everything he has to the earth through his right hand connected to the stalactite. He wears green layered over yellow because he does not allow his mind to look beyond his devotion to labor.

IN A READING: This card could represent a person (male or female) or a situation. The person is a well grounded, constant, dependable, and slow to change. He believes in the value of hard work and gives everything to his job. In a situation questions revolve around employment. Discernment is required to know what changes need to be made. Is your work productive? This card could also indicate the need for grounding or stability.

MEDITATION: I draw upon the stability of the Earth to ground me.

DAILY READING: Take a day off to evaluate your focus and where changes need to be made.

Mother of Earth

Growth requires nurturing.

Primary Concepts: Nurturing, Fertility

Description: The Mother of Earth shows a zoo worker feeding a bottle to a baby polar bear. She is in the bear's habitat and lovingly holds him on her lap while feeding him. The white habitat has a geometric design and there is an opening looking out to the exterior environment. She wears green scrubs with yellow and brown shoes.

Commentary: This card represents the very best part of all of us, our ability to give unconditional love. The Mother of Earth is sharing her love and warmth. She volunteers to do this work because she knows how important and vital it is to give of herself. It is cold here in the bear's habitat but she is not concerned about her own comfort, only that of the baby bear. Nurturing helps us grow. Without it we cannot survive. The infant cub represents fertility and growth. The womb-like geometric design of the habitat symbolizes the building blocks of life. Her green scrubs stand out like the persistence of life in the harshness of winter. Her shoes represent a balance of mind and body.

In a Reading: This card could represent a person (male or female) or a situation. The person loves nature and all creatures. She takes care of everyone and offers assistance to anyone in need. Sometimes she compromises her own well being in the process. In a situation this is a fertile time period. Whatever you give your attention to will grow and thrive. This abundance could come in the form of the birth of an actual baby or of an idea, plan, or project. Don't exclude your own needs.

MEDITATION: I connect to nature and find myself.

DAILY READING: Give birth to a new idea today, nurture it and it grows.

FATHER OF EARTH

What is grounded endures.

PRIMARY CONCEPTS: Abundance, Endurance

DESCRIPTION: The Father of Earth shows a rancher standing at the top of a long stone staircase looking out over all he owns. There are snow covered mountains, trees, and horse barns. Horses are making their way to the pasture. His hands are on his hips. He wears green and blue with cowboy boots and spurs.

COMMENTARY: The Father of Earth has built his domain through his own hard work and sacrifice. His pose suggests he is well satisfied with what he sees. He takes what the Earth has to offer but gives back equally so there is never a shortage of resources. Like the mountains, what he has built will endure for generations. This card shows how we cultivate abundance in our lives. Respect the source, the

Earth, and never take more than needed or take by unscrupulous means. Then replace what was taken by giving back in equal share. This ensures stability, endurance, and continued growth. The staircase represents his climb to the top. Snow represents the purity of his intent. He wears green to signify his connection to the Earth and prosperity. Blue suggests he finds peace in what he does. Spurs represent the motivation to prosper.

IN A READING: This card could represent a person (male or female) or a situation. The person is a hard worker who creates abundance. He appreciates the natural environment and draws strength from it. This person is not complex but stable, grounded, and very practical. In a situation this card represents growth and abundance. Enjoy what your hard work has accomplished. The abundance you create at this time endures.

MEDITATION: I give and receive equally.

DAILY READING: Be satisfied with what you have and you will always have enough.

Layouts

ONE CARD READINGS

```
┌─────┐
│ 1   │
│     │
│     │
└─────┘
```

Each card within the Tarot deck contains a great deal of information that can be perceived on multiple levels. You may find many instances where one card is sufficient to answer your question. In addition to general questions, here are some unique uses for one card readings.

CARD OF THE DAY READING

One of the most common uses for one card readings is picking a card to forecast the day ahead. This reveals the theme or tone of the day. It also points out potential pitfalls or advantages to be aware of. A card of the day reading is included with each card description in this book.

WHERE IN THE WHEEL READING

Throughout our lives we are continuously moving through cycles of growth. Discovering more about where you are in the current cycle can be helpful. Begin by separating all of the Key cards from your deck. Shuffle them well and then pick one at random. This card's placement within the order of Keys will give you an indication of where you are in the current cycle. The Key's description can give more clarity to what you are experiencing. You can also refer to the story of the Traveler's Journey in the Introduction to the Keys.

Reading for an Expectant Parent

Get a glimpse into the personality of a baby on the way. Divide the four Child cards from the rest of the deck and randomly choose one. All of the Child cards can represent males or females. You may not be able to determine the sex of the child but you can discover characteristics and personality traits of the baby to be.

A New Beginning

Are you about to start a new job, make a move, or begin a new adventure? This is a way to find out more about it. Separate the four Ones from the deck. Chose one at random and get insight into what kind of new beginning this will be.

Three Card Readings

Three card readings are an excellent way to start learning the Tarot. There are fewer positions to remember and you can begin to see how the cards relate to one another in a layout.

Answering Questions with Three Cards

This layout can be applied to any type of question.

POSITION ONE: The past. These are the events and experiences leading up to the question and the basic underlying factors.

POSITION TWO: The present. This is what is happening right now, defining or influencing the question.

POSITION THREE: The future. What is likely to happen if no changes are made or what changes need to be made for a different outcome.

THE LOVER'S TRIANGLE

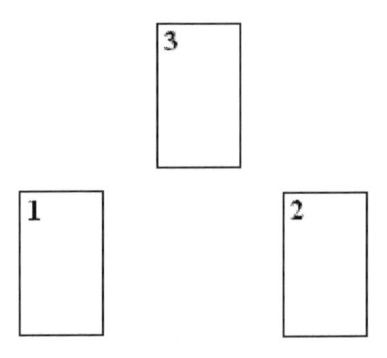

This is a snapshot of the current or potential relationship at the time of the reading or why a past relationship failed.

POSITION ONE: This is you within the relationship. It is how you see it and your role within it.

POSITION TWO: This is your partner's role within the relationship and how you perceive their role.

POSITION THREE: This position represents the status of the relationship at this moment in time. It is what brought you together or what the union is based on.

THE MONEY TREE

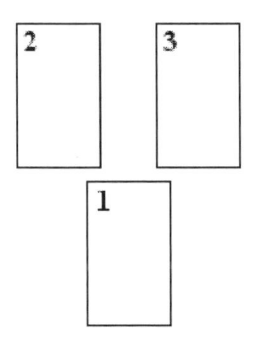

This is a quick overview of your financial situation.

POSITION ONE: This describes your current finances. It is also the status of your present career.

POSITION TWO: This is what needs to happen to improve your financial situation. It is opportunities to take advantage of or pitfalls to avoid.

POSITION THREE: This is the financial outlook moving forward. It may indicate new careers, opportunities for investment, or the general status of your finances.

THE PILLAR OF HEALTH

```
    ┌───┐
    │ 3 │
    │   │
    └───┘

    ┌───┐
    │ 2 │
    │   │
    └───┘

    ┌───┐
    │ 1 │
    │   │
    └───┘
```

The Tarot should never take the place of a trained medical professional; however some of the most often asked questions are about health. The following layout offers a glimpse into the wellbeing of the client. The cards can suggest ways to improve health in a specific area or indicate good health. They may also point out problems to avoid, changes to make, or areas where more attention is needed.

POSITION ONE: Physical. This includes the body of the client and their physical environment.

POSITION TWO: Mental. This covers the mind, thoughts and emotions of the client.

POSITION THREE: Spiritual: This includes the spirituality of the client. Everything we come into contact with physically, mentally, and emotionally begins in the spiritual realm. This position could indicate a problem before it becomes manifest in the physical.

THE STEPS TO ENLIGHTENMENT

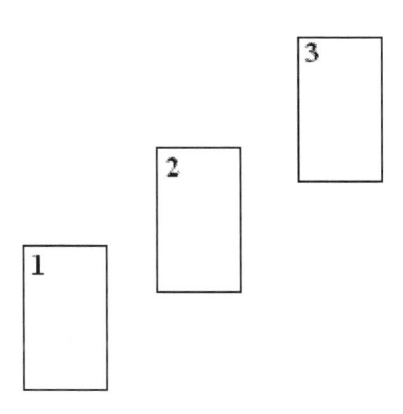

Spiritual insight exists all around us. The Universe never stops providing guidance. The Tarot can help us understand what steps we need to take in order to move forward on our path in a positive direction. This layout provides an arrow to point the way.

POSITION ONE: Embrace or release. This position indicates what you need to either accept into your life or let go of for self improvement.

POSITION TWO: Action. This is the next step you need to take. It is a physical act you must carry out.

POSITION THREE: Insight. This card is a sign from the Universe. It could be a gift, a direction, or a new truth.

Today's Celtic Cross

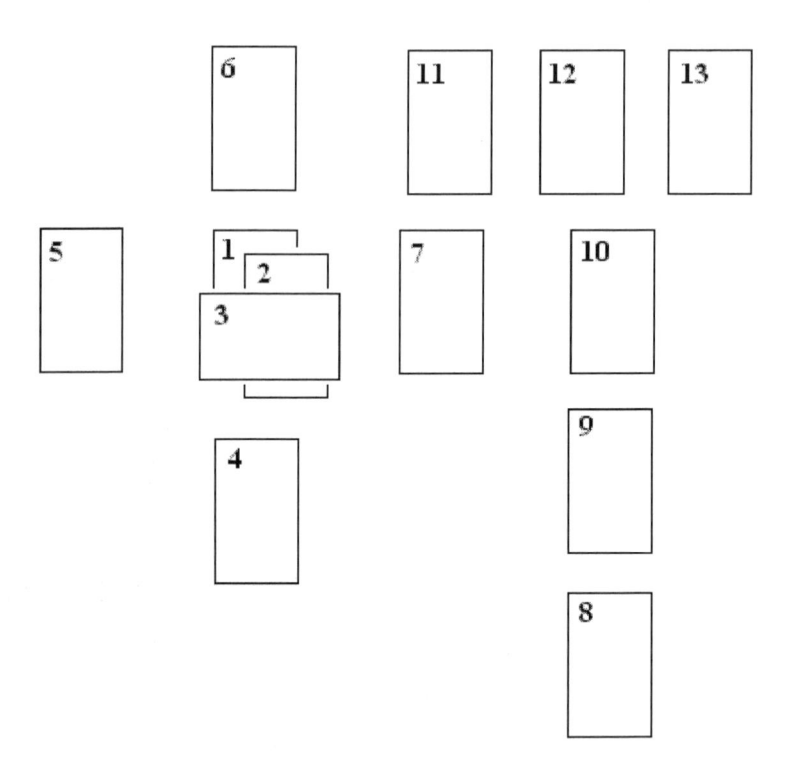

The Celtic Cross is one of the most popular and functional layouts. It is designed to give an overview of the client's life and provide probable outcomes. Expanding Dimensions has added two cards to the traditional ten card spread and updated the positions. The two additional outcome cards offer more information for an expanded view of the future.

Position One: Now. This card represents what is going on right now in the client's life or what is currently on their mind. It is the problem, question, or situation they want answers for.

Position Two: Influence. This card is the atmosphere surrounding the client and their question at the moment. It is the setting of the stage.

Position Three: Opposition. This is an obstacle which must be overcome to move beyond the current situation.

Position Four: Foundation. These are the past experiences which are influencing the present situation. It can also represent the subconscious mind or past lives. This is what led to this moment.

Position Five: Recent past. This position indicates something which has recently occurred. It contributed to the current situation. It may be so recent it is still unknown.

Position Six: Expectations. This is the expected outcome or ideal. It reflects the client's beliefs, positive or negative. It may or may not occur.

Position Seven: Near future. This position indicates something that is about to happen or an influence about to enter the client's life.

Position Eight: The client. This card describes the client at this moment, their attitudes, reactions, and how the situation is affecting them.

Position Nine: Environment. This position represents influences and opinions surrounding the client. This could include family, friends, coworkers, or actual environments such as home, or workplace.

POSITION TEN: Hopes and Fears. This indicates the unconscious true desires and suppressed fears that are influencing the outcome of the situation. Often what is hoped for is also feared.

POSITIONS ELEVEN, TWELVE, AND THIRTEEN: Future. This is the direction the client's life is taking. The blending of these three cards is the most likely outcome of the current situation if no changes are made.

TODAY'S JOURNEY TAROT SEVEN CARD MERKABA SPREAD

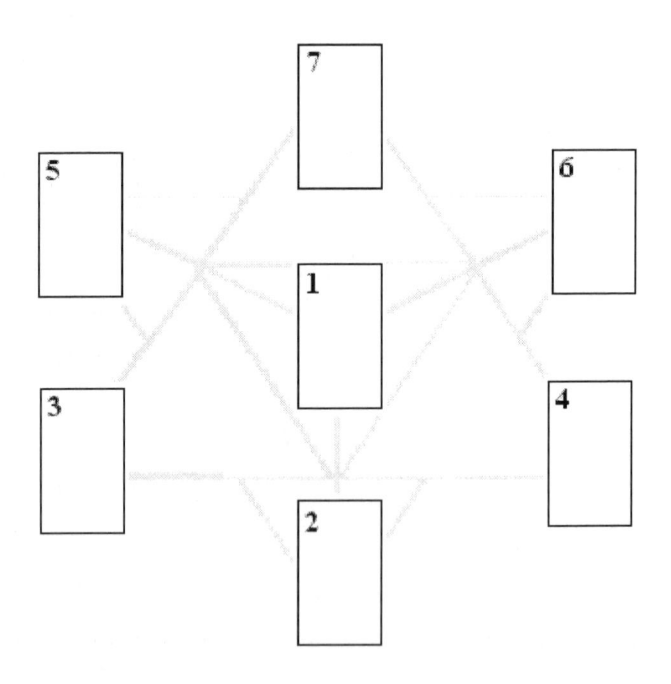

Today's Journey Tarot cards can be used with any layout, but the Seven Card Merkaba Spread was created by Expanding Dimensions to focus on a single issue, question or situation. The Merkaba and the Tarot are vehicles to enlightenment.

POSITION ONE: Essence. This position is the theme of the reading identifying the central question or situation. It defines the issue. This position describes what is going on right now in the client's life and focuses on that concern or question.

POSITION TWO: Experience. This is how the past is now affecting the Essence. The events revealed in this position may have recently occurred or may have happened so long ago that they are no longer remembered but are still impacting the client.

POSITION THREE: Influence. This is what is presently influencing the person, situation or course of events. It is the environment or energy around the client. This could include where they live or work. It could also include the influence of family, friends, or coworkers and their attitudes, opinions and beliefs.

POSITION FOUR: Opportunity. This is the growth offered through opportunities which are about to enter the client's life. This is the near future. This could be an obstacle to overcome or a positive event to take advantage of. It is up to the client whether or not to accept the opportunities.

POSITION FIVE: Potential. These are the probabilities if action is taken and the growth offered in Position Four is accepted. It expands the Opportunity into new possibilities.

Position Six: Progression. This card is the result of your growth. This is the new path you are creating. It is the movement toward Manifestation.

Position Seven: Manifestation. This position is the outcome where the new path you are creating leads.

Reading the Tarot

Reading the Tarot

A reading can cover any area of life: spiritual, relationships, career, family or health. Make a story out of your reading by linking the cards together and describing what the cards mean to you. Usually your first impression is the best interpretation. The cards will address the question or issues and how that situation is likely to turn out. They will also express the positive and negative influences around the situation which should be addressed. The cards are not absolute. Everyone has free will to change their future by making a different decision today. What you are predicting is the probable outcome if no changes are made. The meaning of the cards is influenced by their position in a layout and the other cards surrounding them. They are not limited to any predetermined definition.

Does the Tarot predict the future?

The future is more flexible than most of us believe. It is always in a process of change. Every decision we make, every action we take alters the path being laid out before us. It is a contradiction to believe we create our own reality and also fate casts a destiny we cannot escape or affect. With the future always in a state of flux how can the Tarot accurately pinpoint things to come? There are two reasons. First there are aspects of the future that can be predetermined because of the predictability of human nature. The second reason is the Tarot offers an expanded, multi-layered view of the critical time period when the future is being created. The way the Tarot works could be compared to a more common and easily understood tool, a road map.

A map allows you to pinpoint your exact location and provides a larger view of your environment. It makes the previously unknown possibilities that lay ahead visible. A map also gives you information about the route you are taking. Possible delays can be avoided and detours can be clearly marked so you can easily get where you want to go. In addition to delays you may want to avoid, a map also suggests points of interest you might want to see to make your journey more interesting. These are options the Tarot provides. Both the Tarot and map offer possibilities but neither can choose what direction to take. That decision is up to you. With every change you make you change your future.

Why are there so many superstitions surrounding the Tarot?

The Tarot has been kept secret for too long. Superstitions grow up around anything kept hidden. The knowledge the Tarot has to teach is taught by other traditions as well. It is not a secret. It's just not readily available, because it has been shrouded in mystery for centuries. Only a select few could retain the knowledge and therefore the power. As we came to believe special training, illuminated wisdom, or psychic powers determined our ability to read the cards, it limited people who believed they didn't have those qualities. Consequently the cards became a fortune telling device instead of the beautiful system of guidance and wisdom they were meant to be.

How should I store my Tarot Cards?

There are many superstitions about how a Tarot deck should be stored. The more practical considerations are the best. Most decks are durable, but after years of use can become worn or even bent. They are a very special tool, and should be treated as such. A sturdy box or bag is essential to keep them clean and protect them from mishaps. The kind of box, color and material of the cloth or bag doesn't matter. Usually the box cards come in deteriorates very quickly if used often and shortens the life of the deck. Some decks, like Today's Journey Tarot come with their own stronger box which is fine. You will often take your cards with you when you travel or to do readings at fairs or parties, so finding a box that fits the size of the deck is preferable to something large or bulky. As long as you are comfortable with the way your cards are stored and they are convenient for use that is the proper way. The material used, the colors, styles and decorations are all up to you.

Why are there so many different Tarot decks? Which one is best?

This is one of the most frequently asked questions from new students of the Tarot. They are confused by the hundreds of different decks on the market. The answer to this question varies from person to person because each deck is designed to appeal to a different type of reader. We may prefer one over the other but only because we connect with the imagery, artwork, style, size or even colors. We may be attracted to a deck and then find its artwork is too obscure or the mythology behind the deck is too much to memorize.

The Tarot is not a deck of cards. It is a concept and philosophy that can be expressed in many ways. The seventy-eight Tarot cards are each unique within a deck, but from deck to deck should express the same general meaning. So the Youth of Fire, no matter what it is called in any other deck, should convey the same council from deck to deck, with only minor differences. In choosing a deck, especially for the first time, it is best to find one you like. Then it helps to ask an experienced reader if this deck would be easy to use. New Tarot students often get frustrated with all of the information they feel they must retain before they can start reading. Some decks are definitely easier than others. Once the basic meaning of the cards is learned, you can move on to other decks.

Why is the Tarot deck divided into two parts?

A traditional Tarot deck is made up of the twenty two cards of the Major Arcana and the fifty six cards of the Minor Arcana. It was long believed the Major Arcana or Keys were the older of the two and that the sections of the deck were combined at some point in history. It was also said the Minor cards or Elements were the ancestors of our modern playing cards. Recent scholars have determined this may not be true. Like so much else about the Tarot we may never know for sure. Many Tarot readers view the Major Arcana, Latin for Greater Secrets, as addressing spiritual issues. They put more importance on these cards. The Minor Arcana, Latin for Lesser Secrets, are said to be about more mundane matters. While it is true the Major Arcana cards embody major spiritual archetypes, everything in existence is spiritual. So while the Minor cards may be addressing whether or not to buy a new car rather than some deep spiritual truth, there is a spiritual lesson inherent in that purchase, or maybe several. A Major Arcana card, like Union, may be addressing a commonplace relationship issue. Look at all of the cards as a spiritual gift of wisdom for maneuvering through life. Who is to say which of these lessons is more important than another?

Do I have to be psychic to read the Tarot cards?

We are all psychic. Some have developed this ability more than others. There are those born with more of an innate gift. It is not unlike learning to play the piano. Anyone can be taught to play. With practice they can become really good. A few people toddle up to the keys at a very young age and begin making their own music. Some play by ear, others must rely on music books. Psychic ability is nothing more than the intuitive part of all of us. Whatever your level you can read the cards. Working with the Tarot enhances our intuitive nature. It is a way we can become more psychic.

How long will it take me to learn the Tarot cards?

The answer to this question is very subjective. Once started, the Tarot is a life's work. It is possible to learn the symbolism or the meaning of the cards, in a relatively short period of time, but that is not all the Tarot has to teach. It is not just a tool to do readings, but a beautiful expression of guidance, wisdom, and spirituality. There are layers upon layers within its seventy eight cards describing everything life has in store for us and the ways in which we can meet these challenges.

What is a good way to learn to read the cards?

Practice with three-card readings at first. No matter what layout you use, the first three cards often define the theme of the entire reading. Lay out three cards over and over again. Ask simple questions, even questions you already know the answer to. At first your reading may be a bit awkward as you read each card's meaning one at a time, but soon you will find yourself being able to read them as a group. One card may stick out as the dominant answer with the other cards as supporting, or all three together will each give equal elements of the answer. As you progress to a full reading with ten or more cards (depending on the layout) it will be easier to see the connection between the cards in their positions. Three cards can also be used to clarify or give further info on the initial reading if you require it. Practice is important.

Is there a ritual to follow for the cards to work?

There is absolutely no particular ritual required for the Tarot cards to work, although many readers do have rituals they swear by. Elaborate rituals, or dependency on specific preparations, will only limit you, not the cards. The cards are always ready to work. It is a matter of having complete trust in them. As soon as they are in your hands, that connection is all you need. Make certain you are in the best frame of mind possible before starting a reading. Focus all your attention on the client. During the reading, it is all about them. All readers develop habits they like to incorporate into their readings. But do not become dependent on those habits. All that is really necessary is you and your cards.

What is the best way to shuffle the cards?

Each individual reader develops their own method for shuffling the cards. One option is to begin shuffling right away when someone comes for a reading while making small talk to put the client at ease. Often people are nervous when they are about to get a reading, not knowing what to expect. After shuffling hand the cards to the client. They can shuffle or cut the cards any way they like. Many readers do not like for other people to touch their cards. It is an old tradition that should be honored if a reader feels that way. Never touch someone else's cards without their permission. However giving the cards to the client achieves two goals. First, it further puts them at ease. The cards seem less threatening if they can touch them. Second, it incorporates their vibrations into the cards and opens them up for the reading. If the client doesn't cut the cards, you can cut them into stacks and intuitively pick the one for the top. Many decks are oversized and require extra effort to shuffle smoothly. It takes practice to shuffle any cards. Professionalism is diminished if your cards fly all over the room when you try to shuffle. It is also a distraction that may keep you from being centered and focused on the client. It may be necessary to use a smaller deck and like everything else associated with reading, practice is essential.

What is the best layout to use for reading the cards?

Like so many other things about reading Tarot, the layout you use is based on what is most comfortable for you. There are many layouts available or you can even make one up yourself. There are some characteristics to look for. How many cards does the layout use? Too many cards in the initial layout can be confusing. It is just too much information you probably won't use. Ten or less positions usually give you a good variety of the cards and plenty of info to work with. Do the positions flow into one another? The positions are usually past, present, future, obstacles, advantages, influences and so on. If the layout is too complicated or does not allow you to tell the story the cards present, it will keep you from getting to the message of the reading. How much space does the layout take up? This is a practical consideration. If you are reading at a desk, your space may be limited. If the layout is so convoluted that it takes a large space, it limits where you can do readings. Learning the seventy eight cards is daunting enough. There is no reason to add a complex layout to that. So, try out different layouts. The one that flows for you is a good place to start!

How do I choose a significator?

The significator is the first card that falls in a layout. It usually identifies the client and begins to define the question or questions surrounding them. Traditionally the reader picks the significator from the Court or Family cards based on the physical characteristics and possibly the personality of the client. If she has blonde hair for example, the Mother of Water might be selected. This method is rather outdated and arbitrary. All of the other cards in a layout are selected at random after the cards are shuffled and cut. You trust this method to give you the cards that are meant to be in the reading. Why should you choose a significator, using your preferences to determine such an important card? You can use the top card as the significator, allowing the cards to make that choice as they do with the rest of the reading. Like everything else with reading the Tarot, each reader should decide what methods they are most comfortable with and what works for them, rather than relying on traditional methods alone.

How long should a reading last?

It is best to gauge the length of the reading by the needs of the client. Some readers use timers or cut clients off when their time is up. People are different. Some will get right to the question or issue, some will take more time to warm up, open up, and let you in. It is the reader's responsibility to give the client every opportunity to find the answers they seek. Sometimes a reading may last just a few minutes and sometimes it can go for over an hour. If a client begins to repeat themselves by asking the same question over and over or the cards have said all they are going to say, end the reading by saying something like, "Unless you have any more questions..." Most people get the hint. The client's welfare and comfort should always be more important than the time on the clock.

Should I use reverse cards in the layout?

It has been a tradition that cards are laid in the way they fall. If they are up side down when turned over, they are laid in the spread that way. This position represents the reverse or opposite meaning of the card, usually the negative. Many readers read that way and of course it is their choice. The members of Expanding Dimensions do not reverse cards. There are two main reasons. First, when a card is turned up side down, most clients think they know immediately that it's not good. Even if they've never read the Tarot, they've seen enough in the media to know that. So it upsets them and puts them on the defensive which makes for a more difficult reading. The other reason is tied to the first one. There is no reason to focus attention on the negative. All of the cards have both positive and negative attributes and it is up to the reader to discern how the card applies.

Can I read the Tarot cards for my spouse and for friends?

When you are first learning to read the cards, friends can be a big help by volunteering to let you read for them, over and over again. But generally, unless you can be assured of your objectivity, reading for boyfriends, girlfriends, spouses, and family members can cause trouble. It takes a lot of discipline and experience to be able to read the cards without inserting your own opinions and judgments. When reading for someone we love, we may unconsciously inject what we've always wanted to tell them, but haven't. It then appears the cards have told them for us. In other words, your opinion about their life choices comes through. Sometimes this can cause hard feelings. Just make sure that in these situations, you both know this can happen before you begin.

Can I read the Tarot cards for myself?

Reading the cards for yourself can sometimes be tricky. It is difficult to remain objective and not project what you wish into the reading. This shouldn't prevent you from using the cards for guidance, however. It is just something to be aware of while you are reading. The Tarot is a fabulous tool for gaining perspective and direction in your life. You can pull a few cards to get insights into a situation or decision. It is a good idea to draw a card for the day. It tells you what influences may be around you, what to watch out for, and what to take advantage of. If you feel the need for an objective opinion though, consult another reader.

How do I ask the Tarot questions?

The Tarot is an unending resource of information. The deck offers its advice without preconceived bias or judgment. It does not have an ego. Positive or negative associations given to the images on the cards are reflections of the reader's personal understanding of the symbolism. What may be positive to one person may not be to another. Keep this in mind when asking the Tarot questions. If you are confused about answers you receive from the cards it may be the way you are asking. Avoid questions that require a judgment from the Tarot, including yes or no. If you have a decision to make and want the Tarot's advice it would be better to lay out a few cards for each choice. Then you would understand more about each outcome and could choose which path you would prefer to follow. The Tarot will not decide for you, but it can illuminate what lies ahead in each direction so you can make an informed decision.

Can I read the Tarot for more than one person at a time?

Reading for more than one person at a time is not recommended except under certain circumstances. A Tarot reading should be private. Often things are revealed that your client would not like to discuss in front of someone else. Also they may be reluctant to bring up their real questions and it might hinder you from saying what you feel if someone else is listening.

The exceptions include best friends. Sometimes people like to have their best friend with them for the reading (perhaps to take notes). Usually best friends already know everything about each other. The other exception is if someone is very uncomfortable getting a reading alone. This happens sometimes when a client recommends you to someone else. Reading for a couple together is strongly discouraged. You would be surprised at the issues that can arise and the unknowns that can be revealed.

Sometimes a group or partnership may seek council on their business or project. That is totally different because it rarely involves personal information.

Do the court cards always represent people?

It is often thought that the Court or Family cards in the Tarot deck correspond to people in the client's life or even the client themselves. The court cards can indeed represent people but they can also indicate a situation in the client's life. The Page of Cups or Child of Water for example, is typically described as a young person or child who is sensitive or emotionally immature. They are usually a budding artist of some sort and require artistic stimulation as they grow. If this card does not represent a person, it indicates there are circumstances in the client's life that could be described in the same manner. Perhaps they have just discovered a hidden talent and are beginning to nurture it or are involved in an immature emotional relationship. All of the characteristics of the Father, Mother, Youth, and Child cards can be transferred to a situation rather than a person. The cards surrounding it in a reading and your intuition will guide you on the best interpretation.

How often should I read for someone?

Many people enjoy getting readings. They may come to you frequently and request you read the Tarot for them. Reading for someone too often only repeats what you have told them before. Unless they are in a particularly tumultuous time in their lives or a major event occurs, wait at least six months before consulting the cards for them again. The events and decisions discussed need time to play out. Otherwise you will find yourself doing the same reading over and over for the same person. This wastes your time as well as theirs and if they are paying for a reading, it is unethical. There is a danger of someone becoming dependent on the cards, or on you. They may wish the cards to make decisions for them and the cards were not designed to do that.

What if I see something bad in the cards?

All of the cards have a positive and negative side, as does everything else. Naturally there will be times when unpleasant or negative things appear. It is your responsibility to disclose what is there. However, it should be done in a way that creates the least harm. Instead of stating something as a fact, state it as a possibility. After all, the future has not yet been written. No one can predict the future as long as human beings have free will to make choices that constantly change their futures. The cards disclose probable future events based on a client's past choices, not absolutes. If you tell someone something negative as an absolute you are creating fear and contributing to that event coming to pass, not to mention some bad karma for yourself. If the client feels they have no option, they may not make different choices that will avoid or at least mitigate the event.

Do Tarot cards predict death?

Anyone can predict a death. Many readers feel it necessary to give this information they perceive they read in the cards. That is one of the reasons so many people are afraid to get readings. The cards themselves do not predict death. There really isn't any reason to. After all, if a death is predetermined, there is nothing that can be done to stop it. If it is not predetermined and people have free will to change decisions that lead up to their death it would be unethical to give them information that would only serve to frighten them. The cards are a tool of guidance and enlightenment, not fear. An accurate prediction of death could just be a fulfillment of the thought planted in the client's mind.

What if the client says that everything I say is wrong?

Sometimes that happens. Of course you can be wrong, but the cards rarely are. Usually when that is the case, the client has closed themselves to what you are saying. Even if what you say doesn't make sense to them right now, it may in the future. If the client is truly unsatisfied, there is only one choice: Stop the reading and refund any payment. It could just be that the two of you don't "click." However you can also take another look at the cards to see if perhaps you have missed something or can interpret them in another way. You can move on to another subject. Perhaps you just haven't hit yet on what they wanted to hear about. The most important thing to remember is that we are all wrong sometimes. Do your best to make amends to the client and move on.

What if I can't read for someone?

It is important to provide the best environment for readings. That means a comfortable place, you in the best frame of mind possible, and prepared to read. You should also do what you can to make the person you are reading for comfortable, be friendly and open, ease the tension with small talk, and have a professional attitude. Even with the best preparations there may be times when you just don't seem to be getting anything from the cards. This usually happens when you are a new reader and rarely as you gain experience. The ethical thing to do in that case is to tell the person you are reading for the truth. "I'm just not getting anything here." Your two options are to pick up the cards, reshuffle and lay them out again or try again another day. That decision should be the client's. If it happens at a fair or event for example, return their money and suggest they consult someone else. Some people are more difficult to read for than others. There will be times when the client intentionally or unintentionally blocks you. Although you should avoid reading when you are ill, there may be times when your energy is low or you are distracted. Just like anything else you do, there will be days when it is easier than others. That is totally normal.

What should I do when people challenge me about reading the Tarot?

Unfortunately it is inevitable that someone will disapprove of your reading the Tarot. It could be friends, family members, or most often total strangers. This attitude comes from ignorance and closed mindedness, and the negative behavior of some Tarot readers. It is impossible to change their minds. Don't try. If someone challenges you, just let them without arguing your side of the issue. It is a waste of time and energy and only causes more bad feelings. The best way to combat this is to act in a professional manner, don't flaunt your Tarot cards at someone who doesn't appreciate them, and always project positive thoughts and energy. Those of us who love the Tarot do not like to hear the old, tired, negative propaganda about them over and over again. Just do not put yourself into a situation where you have to listen to it. Surround yourself with others of like mind. Change the world by your example.

Tarot Reader Code of Ethics

The Reader shall strive at all times to give the best reading possible.

Always be professional. Do not make a client wait. You and your cards should be ready when a client arrives. You should have a comfortable place for reading and put the client's welfare above all else. All of your attention and focus should be on the client. Patiently and thoroughly answer any and all questions. Know your cards. Practice reading on friends and volunteers. If you change decks, make certain that you have studied them and are comfortable reading with them. Keep studying and learning about the Tarot. There is always more to learn.

The Reader shall use the Tarot as a spiritual tool, staying positive and uplifting.

Never, I repeat never try to elicit an emotional response from your client. It is not your job to frighten or shame them or make them sad. Everyone you read for should feel hopeful and positive after their reading. They should leave you feeling better than when they arrived. You should offer encouraging suggestions and solutions to their problems without judgment. There is always a way to use tact and compassion no matter what the client's problems may be.

The Reader shall refrain from manipulating the Client or using the reading to fulfill the desires of the Reader.

Perhaps you know someone well enough that you have opinions about decisions they should make or how they should live their lives. Ordinarily you would keep these to yourself unless the person asked you your opinion. If this person came to you for a reading it could be viewed as the perfect opportunity for you to tell them what you thought in the guise of the cards revealing this information to them. That is unethical. Even if you have opinions or beliefs different than what the cards indicate, it is your responsibility to **only** disclose information that comes from the cards. It is possible that your opinions and beliefs would unconsciously flavor the reading, but that should be avoided as much as possible.

Of course you never suggest that a client return for more readings to fulfill some needed ritual that will relieve them of their problems. That too is unethical.

Never read for someone you are personally acquainted with (family, friends, etc.) in order to manipulate them to your way of thinking or get them to do something that benefits you.

The Reader shall always respect the rights and the welfare of the Client.

We have already touched on the welfare of the Client in other Codes. The most important are making sure that the client is comfortable at all times and you do not do or say anything that would upset them.

The rights of the Client include their right to refuse what you say. Do not insist that you are right, you may not be. It is their reading. They have the right to interpret what you say in their own way. They also have the right to refuse your advice or not act on it. Many clients return with the same issues time and time again. The cards suggest ways to alter or even alleviate these issues but for whatever reason, the client does not act. That is their right. All you can do is the best you can do to propose the course of action outlined by the cards. The rest is always up to them.

The Reader shall refrain from reading due to physical, mental or spiritual imbalance.

What this means is you should avoid reading when you are not at your best. If you are sick, tired, distracted by your own problems, grieving or emotionally upset in any other way it is best not to do a reading. Your own issues will bleed into the reading and it may not serve as the best council for your client. The only exception is if you are able to **completely** put your own concerns aside.

The Reader shall honor and respect all confidences received and not use the Tarot to invade the privacy of another.

A Tarot Reader is not unlike a doctor or other form of counselor. Whatever is told to you by the Client in confidence should not be repeated as gossip or information to someone else. It is unethical to ask the Client for private information that has no significance to the reading or just to satisfy your own curiosity. It is also unethical to use the cards to try to find out information the Client does not readily provide. If the reading goes somewhere the Client is uncomfortable with, do not force the issue. Change directions and provide whatever guidance is within their comfort level. It is not your job to elicit confessions or uncover secrets.

The Reader shall keep all information received from a reading private; unless permission from the Client has been given or the intention is made clear that a violent crime is about to be committed.

No matter how interesting, juicy, or scandalous it is you do not repeat anything someone tells you in a reading. Even if they tell you they are having an affair with your best friend's husband. Your reputation as a reader is in jeopardy if you are known to repeat what is told to you in a reading. If you suspect someone is going to tell you something you'd rather not hear about, you can decline to read for them and recommend someone else. If it is revealed to you a crime is about to be committed or has been committed, or if someone's life is in danger, you have the same responsibility as any other citizen to notify appropriate authorities.

The Reader shall conduct the reading in private unless otherwise specifically requested by the Client.

Besides the obvious reasons of privacy, there are other important considerations for doing a reading in private. It can be very distracting if someone else is present. They can actually influence the reading by their body language or by interrupting and offering their own advice or suggesting what the client should ask. It is sometimes difficult to uncover the client's needs and questions. The reading then becomes more about what the other person wanted them to hear. Also the client may be reluctant to disclose information with someone else present and you may hesitate to bring up certain issues in front of someone else. This results in a less than honest reading.

The Reader shall recommend qualified professional services whenever the question or problem warrants.

Tarot readers are not doctors, psychologists, lawyers, or any other number of professional people (unless you are, of course). While we may have insight into how problems should be solved, there are many times when our best advice is to seek other help. Only give the client what you are qualified to give. The same would be true if they are seeking astrological information and you are not an astrologer. Do not let ego keep you from referring and recommending your client get the help they need.

The Reader shall accept that the Client has free will and is responsible for his/her own behavior.

While you are responsible for what you tell someone you are reading for, you are not responsible for how they act upon what you say. The exception is if you were manipulating them to act in a certain way. If so, whatever happens to them is your karmic responsibility. If they interpret the information from the reading in such a way that creates negative behavior, and you did not intend it that way, or negative results, then it is their responsibility. In other words, all you can do is honestly interpret the cards and tell the client what they say. It is always up to each individual to make the choices that determine their life.

Meditating with the Tarot

Meditating with the Tarot

Meditation with the Tarot is very helpful for beginning readers. It is a great way to learn and understand the deck. For those who have been reading for a while, it delves into new layers of awareness of the Tarot's philosophy and deeper meanings. One method is to choose a symbol or person from one of the cards and hold that image in your mind while you meditate. See what associations may come to you, how you feel about the symbol, what meaning is revealed. Another way is to imagine you in one of the cards. See yourself in that environment and perhaps even extend it as you look around. This is especially helpful for cards that are difficult for you to learn or remember or you just don't understand.

When you meditate the conscious part of your mind becomes relaxed allowing the subconscious to become dominate. It is this intuitive part of your mind that responds to the Tarot's symbolic imagery. This makes meditation and the Tarot a powerful combination for personal discovery and a deeper understanding of the cards themselves. Each card offers multiple opportunities for use in meditation. You might consider contemplating a card's name, number, a specific color, or one of its primary concepts.

Tarot Affirmation Meditation

In the sections of individual cards each card has been assigned a meditation that corresponds to its meaning. The following meditation is one example of how these powerful affirmations can be used. After you have chosen a meditation spend some time making yourself comfortable and becoming relaxed. Take a few deep breaths in and out slowly. Repeat the statement four or five times in your mind. Continue to relax and ask yourself the following questions. How does this statement relate to my life? Are there specific areas of my life where this applies more than others? When I contemplate this statement what images or scenarios come into my mind? What changes would I need to make in my life to incorporate this statement into it? What impact will internalizing this statement have on my life?

Spend a few more minutes considering the statement. Close your eyes and visualize the positive changes it will create in your future. When you are ready open your eyes.

Entering a Card Meditation

Meditation can provide expanded insight into Tarot symbology. For a unique experience you can place yourself within a card's imagery and interact with its environment. Pick a card or have the deck chose by randomly selecting one.

Get into a comfortable position and begin to examine the card you have chosen. Try to take in as much detail as possible. Close your eyes and picture the card in your mind. Imagine it getting bigger and bigger until the card's border is the size of an average doorway. Now imagine yourself stepping right into the picture. Allow the images to come to life and expand the environment beyond the card's border. Look around. What do you see? What do you hear? You can interact with people in this world. You can touch, handle, move, and manipulate objects here. Spend some time exploring this world. Ask questions. See what else is happening or what happens next. When you feel you have seen all you can, again find the border of the card. Step through to this moment and allow the card to return to normal. Take a few minutes to reflect on what you have experienced and when you are ready, open your eyes.

THE KEY 11 EXPERIENCE MEDITATION

Here is example of how the above mediation might be experienced. Pull Key 11 Karma out of the deck and focus your attention on it for a few minutes. Allow yourself to get comfortable and imagine that you step through the card's border into an auditorium. You are seated in the dark room waiting for the performance to begin.

The room is silent. The audience sits in anticipation. The only light illuminates the thick red curtain. Two dancers emerge at opposite ends of the stage; one dressed in black the other in white. They begin to slowly dance toward one another, but it looks more like seeing one performer dancing in front of a mirror. Like an echo each intricate position is being duplicated move for move. This is the personification of cause and effect or give and take in perfect balance. One is the shadow of the other. As the dancers approach the center of the stage a yin/yang symbol appears there. Gradually they embrace one another. All movement stops when they embody the symbol. The audience is seeing something more than just a performance; something special, even spiritual. After a few silent moments the standing ovation begins. You are left to wonder if you lived with such balance and grace would your life look this beautiful.

Spend a few minutes reflecting on what you have experienced and when you are ready open your eyes.

Elements Family Reunion Meditation

You have been invited to the Today's Journey Tarot Elements Family Reunion. Separate the Family cards from the rest of the deck. Spend a few minutes looking them over. Get into a comfortable position. Visualize yourself arriving at the ranch of the Father of Earth. Your first impression of this expansive property is it is well taken care of and larger than you expected. Even the barns are immaculate. The Father of Earth greets you on the front porch. He waves and welcomes you to his home. Some of the guests have already arrived. The Mother of Water is busy arranging the food on picnic tables. She is focused on her work, not drawing attention to herself. The Youth of Air races by on a galloping horse. She seems to be enjoying herself. You notice the Child of Fire sitting on the porch swing engrossed in his cell phone. The Child of Earth is taking notes for her genealogy project. The Father of Water is talking with everyone and listening intently to all of their problems. He sympathizes and gives gentle support. The Youth of Earth offers to take you on a tour of the property. He's very excited about this opportunity to share his knowledge of the land. The Mother of Fire suggests you might want to do this a bit later and proceeds to tell you about her latest project. All eyes seem to be on her except for the Mother of Earth who is sneaking off to the stables to see the newborn colt. She quietly encourages the children to follow her. The Father of Air has just arrived and immediately begins discussing his ideas for converting the ranch to solar energy. The Child of Water is lying on the grass near the picnic tables, dreamily gazing into the sky. His daydream is abruptly interrupted by the arrival of the Youth of Fire who roars in on his motorcycle. He drops a bag of chips on the picnic table and takes off for parts unknown. The Mother of Air is outraged and begins to loudly criticize his behavior and his upbringing. The Child of Air is trying to get her kite aloft but is so interested in all that is going on she's not getting it into the air. The Youth of Water pays no attention to what anyone else is doing. He is charming a group of girls who are hanging on his every word. The Father of Fire is the last to arrive. He brings a case of champagne to celebrate his latest business acquisition. It looks like the food is ready, so you make your way to the picnic tables to enjoy the feast. Stay and mingle a while. Interact with the characters and ask them questions. Is there any one you feel drawn to or hesitant to meet? When you are ready you can return to this moment.

Today's Journey Tarot Merkaba Meditation

Begin by getting comfortable and allowing yourself to relax. Focus your attention on the merkaba symbol on the back of the Today's Journey Tarot cards. Notice how the two pyramids merge together. Run your eyes along their edges. Relax your body. Imagine you are sitting with your legs crossed in a classic meditation pose. You are comfortable and at ease. Visualize a pyramid of light rising up from beneath you, pointing upward. It moves through the ground, floor, and your body until it stops with you enclosed in its center. You feel an uplifting movement of energy within your body, mind, and spirit. A part of you is reaching out to the Universe. You see a second pyramid of light moving toward you from somewhere high above, pointing down. It easily moves through your body and comes to rest with you at its center. You are in the middle of the merkaba. You feel as if your reach upward has been met by a higher force or vibration. It is here where physical and spiritual energies join. You can feel the power of this union. Its balance creates expanded awareness. It brings new opportunities for creativity, intuition, and guidance. Be open to this wisdom. Now that you have established this link it will continue to illuminate you. It will not dissipate. This is a point of transition that will manifest positively in every aspect of your life. Spend a few more minutes here in this vehicle of transformation. When you are ready you can return to the present moment.

Numbers, colors, and Symbols

Numbers, Colors, and Symbols

Numbers

In a well designed Tarot deck, everything on every card has significance, including colors, numbers, and symbols. Generally the numbers on the Tarot cards correspond to the basic meanings of Numerology. For example, five is a number of change, so all of the fives in the deck could indicate that change is influencing the situation. If more than one five falls in a layout the influence becomes even stronger. Learning more about the meaning of numbers enhances the input of information coming from the cards. Sometimes when the symbols in the cards seem vague, you can rely on numbers to help clarify what they are saying. Double digit numbers are added together to arrive at a single number. For example, ten becomes a one.

Zero - The powerful moment in time just before action is taken, the pause before the leap

One - The self, where power of creation resides, a new beginning or fresh start

Two - Cooperation and partnership, a choice or decision

Three - Number of creation or creativity, self expression, artistry, and imagination

Four – Stability, the strength and endurance of the physical world

Five - Humanity's flexibility and freedom to change, movement

Six - Harmony and relationships

Seven - The analytical mind and potential development of inner resources of meditation and spiritual awareness

Eight - Success, power, and material freedom, authority and leadership

Nine - Pure intellect and initiation, completion or end of a cycle

COLORS

The colors in the cards, background, clothing, animals, flowers, and virtually everything is conceived to add meaning. Colors can give additional information if the symbolism seems vague or hard to understand. Most of us already know a lot of color meanings. For example, pink for love or white for purity. Red is passion and energy and so forth. If colors speak to you, it is worth adding this knowledge to your study of the Tarot. Once you understand more about the meaning of colors it is easy to apply. A man wearing a white coat may represent an innocent, someone who is naïve about the world. A man in a red coat could be more of a rascal, someone who is passionate about what he wants and goes after it. If you disagree with a particular color meaning we suggest always go with your interpretation. You are the one reading the cards.

Black - Entire color spectrum without light, protection, isolation, grounding

Blue - Healing, emotion, subconscious, peace, element of Water

Brown – Earth, grounding, stability, endurance

Gold - Spirituality and power, the Sun

Gray - Doubt, hesitation, limitation

Green - Growth, prosperity, and balance, element of Earth

Indigo - Devotion and intuition, higher levels of consciousness

Orange –Warmth, creativity, and emotions, sociability

Pink - Love and purity

Purple - Worldliness, royalty, and mastery

Red - Energy, passion, strength, and power, element of fire

Silver - Creative imagination, intuition, the Moon

White - Entire color spectrum with light, purity, cleansing, innocence, truth

Yellow - The mind, learning and teaching, intellect, joy, element of Air

Symbols

A symbol tells an idea, fact, or stands for something else. Anything can be a symbol. Some symbols are the same for everyone. A smile always means friendliness. There are also personal symbols. These are special to individuals. For people who love dogs a dog would be positive, but if you were afraid of dogs it might represent fear. There are no right and wrong meanings for symbols. We use symbols in everything we do. It is just another form of language. The classic Tarot deck is filled with esoteric symbolism that is sometimes difficult to understand. Expanding Dimensions chose to use modern symbolism in Today's Journey Tarot. It is easy to relate to the contemporary imagery.

Air - The mind, intellect, abstract thought, and knowledge

Arch - Threshold, point of crossing, passage of change

Birds - Messengers, guides, ability to see clearly

Books - Learning, knowledge, curiosity

Candle - Hope, celebration

Cat – Instinct, seeing what others cannot

Cars - Vehicles of movement, journey, control

Circle - Eternity, cycles, karma

Cup - Emotions, water

Dirt - Foundation, grounding, stability

Dog - Companion, natural world

Dolphin - Moving forward, gentleness, innocence

Dome - Power, authority

Earth - Balance, growth, abundance

Feet - Foundation, understanding

Fire - Passion, energy, strength, ambition

Gate - Passageway, transition, protection

Grass - Growth

Hands - Left hand receives and the right hand gives

Horse – Power, freedom, abundance

Lamps – Source of illumination

Lemniscate – Infinity

Locks – Protection, fear

Merkaba – As above so below, vehicle of transcendence

Moon – Emotions, intuition, creativity, subconscious

Pennants – Symbolic conveyance

Pleiades – Influence for awakening consciousness

Rain – Emergence of emotion

Sea – Depth of emotion

Sign – Message, information, direction

Stone – Strong foundation, manifestation

Sun – Physical, analytical, active, conscious

Torch – Victory, leadership

Water – Emotions, depth, flow, unconscious

Wood – Strength, flexibility, reliability

Window – Point of view

Yin/Yang – Balance, harmony, karma

BIOGRAPHIES

About Expanding Dimensions

Expanding Dimensions, was formed in 2003, and is comprised of five members whose combined knowledge of the Tarot encompasses nearly a century of experience. They coauthored Today's Journey Tarot which was published by Schiffer Publishing in 2011. In order to continue their journey and help others with the Tarot they felt a need to continue exploring Today's Journey Tarot with this guidebook. More information on Today's Journey Tarot can be found at todaysjourneytarot.com.

Teresa Sue McAdams, Bonnie Taylor,
Ben Perry, John Lavey, Pat Lavey

John Lavey began his interest in the esoteric during his extensive study of religion at a catholic school, Flaget High School located in Louisville, Kentucky. John continued the study of religion through his college years at Western Kentucky University. He began studying the Tarot twenty years ago and has read professionally. John lives in a small rural community near Louisville, Kentucky with his wife, daughter, and dog, Brodie. He enjoys long walks in the woods.

Pat Lavey co-authored Today's Journey Tarot with her spouse John and the other members of Expanding Dimensions. Over twenty years ago her interest in the Tarot began in order to understand psychic events which had occurred in her life. Pat has read and taught the Tarot enjoying the experience of giving others the help the Tarot offers. She graduated from Indiana University and has enjoyed diverse careers. Pat takes solace in her rural home in Indiana believing, "Nature always wears the colors of the spirit."- Emerson

Teresa Sue McAdams, Ph.D. earned a doctorate of Philosophy in Parapsychic Science. Sue is a full time teacher of Tarot, meditation, spiritual development and tai chi. It was in Sue's classes that the members of Expanding Dimensions met. She is the author of *Lessons: The Wisdom Within Each Moment*. Sue has worked professionally as a tarot reader since 1988, doing private readings, psychic fairs and events. She is married to co-author Ben Perry.

Ben Perry is the author of *Journeys: A Guide to Group Meditation*. He is the creator of benperrymeditations.com a resource website for his meditation CDs, downloads, books and more. It includes meditations for children, groups, behavior modification and new age. Ben has been reading Tarot and teaching and leading meditation since 1988 and has given lectures at area schools, churches, books stores and learning centers. Ben and Sue live across the river from Louisville, Kentucky with their two cats, Thai and Lily.

Bonnie Taylor is a Reiki Master who has dedicated herself to the healing arts. Bonnie holds a B.S. degree in Architectural Drafting and History and has spent the last twenty years enhancing her knowledge of metaphysics. During the course of her study, Bonnie became interested in the Tarot and has participated in psychic fairs and events. Bonnie meditates regularly and is a 1st Degree Black Belt in Tae Kwon Do. She lives in Louisville with her dog, Maya.

About the Artist

Christopher Wilkey is an illustrator, graphic designer, and muralist, who holds a B.F.A. in Studio Art and an A.A.S. in Computer Graphic Design, as well as having majored in Art at Louisville's duPont Manual Magnet High School. He has been pursuing drawing consciously since the age of seven. A student of Art History, he has found influence in wide ranging movements and artists throughout, but Pablo Picasso, Salvador Dali, M.C. Escher, Alberto Giacometti, and Alex Grey count among those by whom he is influenced. He first encountered information on the Tarot as a child in a book from his family's library that dealt with psychic and esoteric phenomena.

Conclusion

From Beginning to Completion another cycle in Today's Journey has passed. May this book and the deck be your companion through the cycles to come and your guide to expanding dimensions.

Made in the USA
Middletown, DE
02 September 2015